Legally
Branded

Legally
Branded

Shireen Smith

AZRIGHTS
MEDIA
LIMITED

First published in the United Kingdom in 2012 by Azrights Media Ltd

Azrights Media Ltd
81-83 Essex Road
London N1 2SF

A CIP for this book is available from the British Library

ISBN: 978-0957174207

Endorsements

Some entrepreneurs may miss out through not knowing how best to protect their ideas. This book is a must have for any budding entrepreneur who wants to understand how to benefit from their ideas.

————Mike Harris
Founding CEO of First Direct and Egg Banking

Handsomely presented, and with a manageable 'feel' to it that gives it an aura of accessibility, *Legally Branded* practises what it preaches: it sends out a clear, concise message to its business readers as to what problems they are going to face and what options they face if they want to avoid or solve them. Seasoned in navigating the choppy waters where innovative ideas, small businesses and the internet converge, Shireen Smith knows her subject – and her readers – and *Legally Branded* gives them firm and valuable guidance.

————Jeremy Philips
Founder of the IPKat blog, IP Consultant at Olswang LLP and Professional Fellow at Queen Mary IP institute

We've had our fair share of difficulties navigating the tricky waters of branding. This kind of guide is exactly what entrepreneurs need.

————Will Critchlow
Co-founder of Distilled, and writer for the Distilled and SEOmoz blogs

A refreshingly written guide through the maze (and minefield) of brand-related law.

————David Abrahams
Managing Director, Brand Mediation

Stunning all inclusive solution for any entrepreneur needing a comprehensive briefing on branding. A 'must' for any start-up.

————Pauline Bickerton
Honorary Senior Visiting Fellow at Cass
Business School and Serial Entrepreneur

An invaluable reference for any entrepreneur, this book is practical rather than academic and will change the way you look at your business. Have it at the ready for when you launch products, brands, websites, or come up with the next big thing.

————Daniel Priestley
Bestselling author of 'Key Person of Influence'

This book explains the often complex issues of business branding and intellectual property law in a clear and simple manner, incorporating many essential and practical considerations not traditionally found in publications of this nature. It is essential reading not only to those thinking of establishing a new business but for anybody already involved at any level in the management of any business organisation.

————Colin Davies
Senior Lecturer in IP, University of Glamorgan

An excellent introduction both to branding and brand promotion and also to the law which surrounds it. There are sections on owning the copyright in your logo and on trade mark registration, topics which are becoming increasingly relevant in an online age.

————Tim Kevan
Creator of BabyBarista blog and books and
Guardian writer

Azrights Solicitors

Azrights Solicitors, sponsors of Legally Branded, are a law firm based in Islington Green. The firm was established in 2005 with the aim of helping online businesses with matters lying at the intersection between Intellectual Property (IP), Technology, and Internet law.

In the increasingly virtual world in which business operates nowadays, every step a business takes has a digital dimension with IP implications. Azrights helps SMEs navigate the law by, among other things, putting in place a strategy to identify and protect IP, and to manage brands online.

From inception, Azrights has been guided by these core principles:

- **be specialists in our field**
- **offer high quality service, with outstanding value for money**
- **commit to client timescales, and meet every deadline**
- **always pioneer the new products and services the market needs**
- **keep to our quotes, and offer fixed prices where feasible**
- **be pro-active, giving clients what they need, not just what they want**
- **use plain English in all of our advice**

This last principle is part of the firm's overarching goal to make IP, technology, and brand law accessible to those who need it. Azrights' motto is *Easy Legal Not Legalese*, because these grey and complex areas can be a struggle to unravel even for professionals, and the firm believes in translating them into clear, practical guidance clients can act on.

There is a long tradition of putting knowledge out there at Azrights, and giving business owners the tools to succeed. Over the years Azrights has published a range of eBooks, webinars and podcasts, given talks, and even launched entire websites devoted to distilling crucial insights out of a dense body of law and commercial know-how.

Azrights' desire to educate by communicating legal principles in easy and simple ways explains its sponsorship of this book. In everything it does Azrights aims to increase understanding, to excite, and to stimulate innovation in business and IP. Thinking outside the box makes it possible to provide exceptional IP and brand law services – find out more at Azrights.com.

As the Internet revolution continues, and businesses operate more and more in a digital and virtual form, IP becomes ever more relevant to all business owners. Reading *Legally Branded* is a good starting point to understanding this complex area of the law.

Please stay in touch by joining the community of business owners who are creating businesses that are founded on solid IP principles.

Shireen Smith

Twitter: @ShireenSmith@Azrights

Facebook.com/Azrights

Weekly blog updates: www.azrights.com/blog

www.azrightstrademarkregistration.co.uk/blog

Contents

Preface

The legal aspects of branding are too important for business owners to neglect, which is why I chose to write *Legally Branded*.

As the Internet revolution gathers pace, and all businesses take on an increasingly digital and virtual form, knowledge of intellectual property (IP) law becomes crucial for business owners and citizens alike. Indeed, I believe an education in IP will become a mainstream subject for school children in the UK within the next ten years. So, I want to communicate the relevance of IP law to the world, and hence decided to write this book.

I love to help business people turn their ideas into a business and a brand. Highlighting the pitfalls and potential dangers ahead helps them to pursue their goals with a higher chance of success, and fewer expensive mistakes.

Whilst I have aimed to make this material as accessible as possible, there is a limit to what can be done, due to the inherently complex nature of IP law. For example, the use of technical terms like 'infringement' is unavoidable. To tackle this, I have provided a glossary at the end of the book for reference.

Essential terminology to be aware of before reading this book

The concept of intellectual property rights (IP rights) can alienate some people as they don't really know what it means. IP is a system of laws governing matters that you can't see and touch (intangibles), and takes the form of rights, the most well known of which are copyright, trade mark, design, and patent. These terms are often confused or misunderstood, leading people to believe a name can be copyrighted or a book patented, and that all ideas put out there by a business are its IP. So, while the glossary contains more detailed explanations, for now it's worth taking on board the difference between the various IP rights. You will then be better placed to know which type of protection your business should pursue.

Copyright is the most universal of rights, covering written materials, music, art, logos, and computer programs, to name a few. Names and slogans can be trade marks if they pass various requirements the law lays down but they are never anyone's copyright. As such trade marks are one of the most important of IP rights to understand in relation to brands. Design rights protect the visual aspects of certain designs, like handbags or shapes of packaging, and it is even possible to get a design registration for a logo. Finally, patents protect inventions.

Reference book

Legally Branded should be thought of more as a reference than something to read cover to cover, and may be dipped into according to your particular needs. For example, if you are interested in reading specifically about trade marks and brand names, refer to Chapters 2, 3, 4, 12, 15, and 16. On the other hand, if you want to focus more on copyright, look to chapters 5 and 7 initially.

It will also be useful to consult the index when searching for particular topics which do not have a dedicated chapter, such as patents.

I have covered a wide array of Internet related subjects in this book because nowadays doing business needs to take account of the online dimension. Among other things the book covers online branding and websites, reputation monitoring and brand building on social media, as well as brand naming strategies, logos, trade marks, copyright and other IP issues. Therefore, this book aims to provide first-port-of-call, accessible guidance to business owners aiming to understand how IP rights impact on their business plans.

Introduction

If you are an entrepreneur or small business owner who wants to access the kind of legal guidance that the world's top brands have on tap from their teams of in-house and external lawyers, then read on.

Once you appreciate the legal issues concerning branding, you'll be able to position your products and services for sustained success. Even if you don't aspire to be a household name, this book will help you avoid a host of common problems and pitfalls in business.

'Brand' is a term that, while attracting interest, can also alienate some small and medium-sized enterprises (SMEs) who may think their business is too small to ever become one. 'Brand' is not simply about the size of a business, but whether a business has a reputation among a group of target consumers for delivering a particular outcome. Also, it's about substance, and some image elements are more important than others and contribute to the brand's competitive advantage. Some small business owners assume their brand is their logo and they can be quite resistant to advice that contradicts this belief.

Even if you believe your business will never be a brand, you'll find this book provides a valuable insight into how you can best protect your company's interests and ensure you stay on the right side of the law. It deals with issues that apply universally to all businesses, whether or not they are brands. For instance, all businesses need to know how their website projects, or choice of domain or company name, might affect them. Businesses that do not have an Internet presence will still need to understand some key online issues about social media, because even if they are not engaging online themselves, their customers certainly will be.

Brand law

Intellectual property (IP) law is relevant to all businesses, because it is the law that governs 'intangibles' – in other words, assets you cannot touch or feel. A brand is an intangible asset. However, IP law is by no means the only area of law that impacts on brands. I prefer to use the term 'brand law' to describe the necessary expertise required by a lawyer advising in this area. As well as IP law expertise, such a lawyer should have solid experience of registering trade marks in order to have a feel for names from both a marketing and a legal perspective. Otherwise, a good grasp of IT, social media and Internet law, as well as an understanding of search engine optimisation (SEO) and domain names, is essential to online branding. A brand lawyer should also have an appropriate understanding of related areas such as employment law, defamation, marketing and advertising.

Enhance your business's success

I've heard prominent entrepreneurs dismiss intellectual property rights (IP rights) as only marginally relevant for service-based businesses, believing that success is solely dependent on 'thought leadership'; in other words, having and communicating innovative ideas and being the 'go-to' expert. But this is not the whole picture, and that's why I have deliberately picked a service-based fictitious business to focus on throughout this book. Business owners will then be able to see why taking account of legal principles enhances their success with the publishing model and supports the business model. It reduces the scope for unfair competition from others, not to mention loss of sales and copyright infringement. I've also highlighted countless other ways in which building on a solid legal foundation is the way to achieve your goals.

At the other extreme are those business owners who are overly mindful of IP rights, to the point of treating them as an end in themselves. Every business should carefully consider how IP rights impact on its goals. Acquiring rights regardless of whether you really need to incur the expense is wasteful. Similarly, refusing to transfer IP rights to others, even where you don't benefit from holding onto the right, such as copyright in a logo, could damage relations with clients for no good reason.

The widespread misinformation about IP rights results in some SMEs neglecting the issue completely. However, all businesses can benefit from considering how IP rights might help them achieve their goals and build assets. By taking a strategic approach to IP, it becomes much easier to decide how to budget for and deal with IP issues that arise on a day-to-day basis.

Setting an IP strategy can be difficult in practice due to the lack of accessible information on brand law. This book will help business owners to gain a fresh perspective on IP, and to understand it sufficiently to decide whether to consult a solicitor for specific guidance.

Why this book is different

Existing books on brand law are written for lawyers and therefore use language and jargon that make them inaccessible to non-lawyers (and sometimes even to professionals). And while there are books on IP law aimed at non-lawyers, such as *Patents, Registered Designs, Trade Marks and Copyright for Dummies* (John Wiley & Sons, 2008), there is nothing specifically written on brand law for business owners, and the advice that is available to them is very patchy. In large businesses, the in-house lawyers take care of the legal aspects of branding, but small businesses don't have this safeguard. This book aims to plug the gap.

Moreover, it's not just business owners who can gain useful insights from this book, but also branding industry and web professionals, investors, corporate and commercial lawyers, business advisers, marketing directors, journalists, students, and so on.

International nature of IP law

Much of the information contained in this book is of universal application, covering such areas as the Internet and social media, and its focus is on general legal principles. IP law is now an international subject as countries have joined forces and signed up to treaties and conventions. The upshot is that business owners in countries other than the UK can benefit from the material in this book and gain an understanding of the issues, even if some of the details of the laws may be more appropriate to an audience subject to English law.

IP law and the legal profession

The current professional legal landscape leaves small businesses poorly served because they often have no input from lawyers on their website and design projects. Consequently, they risk infringing on others' rights, wasting time and money acquiring weak branding, or losing money through failed website projects.

The solicitors' section of the legal profession regards IP rights as a specialist subject. This means high-street law firms who advise business start-ups are not equipped to include advice on simple copyright and legal issues affecting website projects, for instance, or choice of business name. Although there are many trade mark and patent attorneys who could advise on names, few small businesses are aware of their existence. Moreover, in terms of brand law, these firms tend to focus on trade mark registration and are unlikely to have the expertise to deal with the range of issues that businesses need help with, such as their website and Internet marketing projects.

For instance, a good client of ours stumbled on our firm by chance when she was searching on the Internet for 'property lawyers' to handle her conveyancing transaction. She had been trading very successfully for six years without being aware that there was such a specialism as IP law.

Keeping abreast of new developments

The growth of the knowledge economy, globalisation, Internet revolution and digital word of mouth are all reasons why brands and IP have become central issues for all businesses, irrespective of size or industry focus. The legal profession has been blindsided by the rapid development of Internet technologies and social media. Consequently, there are not enough solicitors and other legal advisers with relevant knowledge of brand law.

Businesses which are just starting up or existing ones that are launching new products or services are often uncertain about what branding involves. As lawyers tend not to discuss such matters with them, businesses often assume that their web designer or other expert knows all the necessary law relating to brands and websites. They don't. That's not their focus or expertise. So, at the very least, business owners need to be aware of the legal issues that impact on their projects, by gaining an insight into such issues themselves. So, if you use an outside agency to help you plan your branding, beware of putting all your confidence in the agency for every aspect of branding.

What agencies don't tell you

Typically, branding professionals working in smaller agencies have cut their teeth on projects for large organisations. In large companies, the legal aspects of branding are taken care of 'in the background', usually before the designers are brought into the project. Names will have been approved, and contracts reviewed or drafted for the company to use when engaging branding and Internet professionals. This way, the company's interests are properly taken care of.

However, with smaller businesses, the danger is that branding agencies tend to assume their SME clients know why they need to involve lawyers and that the legal issues will get taken care of separately. They may not realise that their role with a small business should involve alerting them to legal points, even if they are the ones who have picked a name for their client. Agencies will not necessarily be any more knowledgeable than their clients about the legal ramifications of certain decisions. Many of the staff receive no training in the law and simply rely on picking up the legal information they need to know. I know this from experience of working with many agencies.

I am often asked to help small business clients to register their trade marks, and advise them on Internet law, social media issues and IT law. Among other things, I help businesses to draft various types of contract, secure ownership of their brand's visual identity and websites, guide them on domain names, defamation laws, privacy and marketing activities, and produce documentation to engage staff and outsource work. This is why my area of expertise is best described as 'brand law' rather than IP law.

The way ahead

In summary, SMEs need to take account of the legal dimension before developing a brand identity. However, an IP lawyer is not necessarily the right type of specialist to help small businesses with their brands. IP law is a vast subject and while IP lawyers have general knowledge of it as a whole, they specialise in different aspects of IP law. In order to assist SMEs with their branding requirements, an IP lawyer would need to be focused on brands, trade mark registration work, copyright and Internet law (including social media).

There are a number of law firms that currently provide the range of services that brand law entails, although they do not label themselves in this way yet. Perhaps it will take the widespread adoption of this new discipline of brand law for small business owners to have access to the type of law firm that would be best placed to help them.

This book is a first step in that direction.

Part One
The Brand Name

Chapter 1

You don't need to be big to be a brand

'Ideas are more powerful than all the armies of the world' Victor Hugo

Ideas are behind every great business or innovation that transforms our lives. Walt Disney is reported to have said, 'if you can dream it, you can do it', and he transformed his dream of creating an amusement park with attractions for children and adults alike into a reality.

Jeff Bezos, founder of Amazon.com, had the vision of selling books online, while Howard Schultz, who built up the successful Starbucks chain, wanted to bring Italian coffee bistros to America. Pierre Omidyar, the founder of eBay, started with the concept of creating an online auction site.

Each of these well-respected and successful companies started with an idea. Before any business plan was drawn up or any details worked out, each company already had firm foundations in a strong vision, a concept and an innovation.

Although ideas are clearly very powerful, the law does not protect a mere idea (more about this in Chapter 8). Former Apple CEO Steve Jobs is frequently described in the media as an 'innovator', 'revolutionary', 'visionary' and 'creative genius' and was essentially known for his ideas. In Apple, he managed to create one of the most greatly admired companies of our times, and its seemingly infinite capacity for innovation has led it to build up a following of admirers. Apple is one of the best examples of the importance of ideas and consistent branding.

If you wonder why the Apples of this world are more inventive, pioneering and successful than their competitors, Simon Sinek's book *Start with Why* (Penguin, 2011) will shed an interesting light on it for you.

Turning an idea into a brand

Whether an idea turns into a great business and brand ultimately depends on how successfully the idea is implemented. That is why potential investors always want to know about the track record of the people behind a business, when deciding whether or not to invest in an idea.

Branding plays an important part in the long-term growth and prosperity of a business, so it's relevant for every small business that aspires to greatness to consider what a brand actually is and what's involved in creating one. However, branding as a subject is itself poorly understood by business owners – and yet it holds a fascination for many of them.

People tend to use the word 'brand' loosely, almost as if it were interchangeable with 'business'. But not every business will achieve brand status in the sense of being well known among its target consumers for delivering on a specific promise and thereby enabling it to derive an additional economic benefit, such as being able to charge more for its products and services.

Yes, it's true that every business has a certain personality, which initially derives from its founder or founders, so one could say that every business and every individual is a brand. However, this would be using the word in its loosest sense.

The elusive brand

My search for a definition of 'brand' revealed strong disagreement between experts, so I decided to ask my contacts to tell me what they understand by the word.

I began by pointing them to the definition by David Abrahams in his book *Brand Risk: Adding Risk Literacy to Brand Management* (Gower Publishing, 2008):

A brand is not a trade mark or reputation. Brands are complex intangibles, whose character is a property that emerges from a blend of attributes, some of them seemingly insignificant. It is the sum of all information about a product, a service or a firm that is communicated by its name. This holds true in industrial and professional markets, where brands can create and project emotional and self-expressive benefits just as they do in consumer markets. Every organisation with an identity therefore has a brand (or brands) that it must manage and protect in order to survive and prosper. A brand can be embodied in a globally advertised symbol. Alternatively, it can be expressed by the renown of partners in a services firm that bears their name.

Here are the various responses I received from business owners, a few of them branding professionals.

- **Your brand is what your customers say you consistently deliver.**

- **Your brand is what people say about you when you're not there. A brand is a promise.**

- **I would argue that a brand is a trade mark or 'reputation' that creates a set of expectations about what the product or service will deliver. A brand is an identity, a set of values embodied in words, logos or otherwise physically represented. A good brand brings customers back. A bad brand, or one that is descriptive or has a negative image, keeps them away. A good brand is built to last. The best things of substance are built to last.**

- **Your brand is the identity that you/your product presents to the rest of the world that creates an understanding/belief/picture in the minds of other people about what it is you will deliver.**

- **A brand is when a big red lorry rolls by bearing the word Costa on it and my three year old points to it and says it's the coffee lorry. Brands go way deeper than the surface they appear on ... Recognisable and meaningful spring to mind. Brand is the embodiment of character (inward) and personality (outward) in a business.**

- A brand is an experience someone has with an organisation across multiple touch points. As Michael Eisner, former CEO of Disney, once said, 'A brand is a living entity – and it is enriched or undermined cumulatively over time, the product of a thousand small gestures'.

- Wally Olins, a thought leader in brands and branding says: 'A brand is simply an organisation, or a product, or a service with a personality ... Branding can encapsulate both big and important and apparently superficial and trivial issues simultaneously ... Branding is not only a design and marketing tool, it should influence everybody in your company, it's a coordinating resource because it makes the corporation's activities coherent and above all it makes the strategy of the organisation visible and palpable for all audiences to see'.

- It is more than personality, more than reputation, more than a promise, it's the distinctive DNA of a business. My personal favourite definition comes from one of my clients based in China, who defines a brand poetically as 'the face and soul of an organisation'.

- To me it's recognition of a product, icon or logo that instantaneously brings to my mind what it stands for, including its value and its values!

- It either draws you toward something or drives you away!

The subject of brands is still in its infancy among business owners and lawyers. People who register trade marks may describe themselves as dealing with 'brands', but that is to use the word in its broadest sense. Brands involve a lot more than trade marks. So, whether you seek guidance from a solicitor who specialises in IP law, or you consult a trade mark agent, you are likely to find that their training has not equipped them to understand the subject of brands in any depth.

In the same way that conveyancing solicitors help people to buy and sell property or resolve property disputes without necessarily knowing very much about property development, it is possible to spend a lifetime practising IP law and registering trade marks without understanding very much about branding.

As someone who is interested in the subject, I've had to rely on my own reading and seek out professional opportunities to educate myself.

Primarily, a brand involves creating a good business that's reliable and known for delivering on a specific promise. This attracts customers who positively want to do business with it rather than with the competition. It also attracts employees, suppliers and, ultimately, investors. So, a brand is not a logo, it's about having pulling power.

Everything you do creates your brand

Think about the associations you have when considering successful brands such as Ikea or Apple. Notice how these names have a reputation for delivering what is often an unspoken promise. In Ikea's case, we expect to find affordable self-assembly furniture when visiting its stores. When we buy Apple products, we expect to get something that's well designed, intuitive and easy to use.

Every brand has its own distinct 'identity' and 'promise'. It's due to this promise that we know to expect something completely different if we buy a Rolex watch rather than a Swatch.

Bear in mind that the overall response a brand evokes is influenced by *everything you do, or don't do,* such as your marketing communications, slogan, employees, packaging, website, videos, photographs, premises and logo. This is by no means a comprehensive list, because many other factors are also involved, including the products or services you sell, the way you respond to telephone enquiries and deal with your customers and the way customers are left feeling.

Other things that contribute to the overall impression about your brand include:

■ **whether you are a virtual business or based in an office**

■ **the way you engage on social media platforms**

■ **whether or not you blog – and if you do, what you write about**

■ **your writing style**

■ **your newsletters and emails**

■ **your physical appearance and that of your staff.**

The trust that your business gradually establishes in return for delivering a particular result or outcome, when customers buy from you, is how your business becomes a brand. Once your business has a reputation that encourages customers to deal with you, your business can be described as being a brand. However, beyond technical performance and fulfilment of basic expectations common to all competitors in the same field, the most resilient brands have an emotional appeal, or one linked to the brand's status (for example, secretly liking using Farrer & Co because they are the Queen's solicitors).

You will be known for delivering a particular quality or outcome because you have consistently and reliably done so in the past. Customers know what to expect if they use your product or service and there's little risk of an unpleasant surprise. Buying a product or service from a business that has not yet acquired brand status is risky, because it represents something untried and untested.

Once a business becomes recognised as a brand, it can command a price premium or a market premium. People are willing to pay a premium to receive the expected results the brand is known for delivering. This applies even if the promise of the brand is based on price. For example, people may still prefer to shop at Ikea rather than at an unknown shop that offers even cheaper prices, because they have certain reassurances regarding product quality and the shopping experience they can expect. They won't have this comfort and recognition if they use an unknown seller. Shopping at Ikea carries little risk because they know what to expect from the brand.

Some small business owners think it's necessary to be a household name or a large business in order to be a brand. But, as the example of Steve Hatt below illustrates, you don't need to be big to have a brand.

Case study: Steve Hatt

Steve Hatt is a small fishmonger in Islington, north London. The shop has been on the same site and operating within the same family for over a century, so it has had time to develop into a brand.

A Google search on its name brings up many reviews about the business, and on reading them it becomes clear that the business is a brand. The visual appearance of the Steve Hatt shop is of a basic fishmonger. It does not have a fancy or elaborate shop design or sign, which you'd expect to see if a business had received branding treatment to promote favourable awareness and stimulate demand for its services.

The shop has a reputation for consistently offering superior-quality fresh fish at value-for-money prices. People travel from far and wide to buy there and there are often queues outside, especially on a Saturday morning as affluent local customers buy fish for their dinner parties. The shop gives good brisk service and has knowledgeable staff who are skilled in preparing fish to your requirements. At the time of writing the shop does not even have a website, proving that it is not designs – such as your logo, business cards or letterheads – that determine whether or not your business has a brand. A business such as Steve Hatt illustrates that the brand is primarily about substance rather than surface imagery.

From this case study it's clear that, while design may help support the overall impression and feelings a brand wants to evoke and convey, if you don't create a successful business that meets a market need, then no amount of 'branding' in terms of visual identity creation will turn your business into a brand. (For more information on the important role that the visual elements play, see Chapter 5.)

An important point to note is that the good associations that customers have with a brand are, for the most part, transferred to the brand's name. Just as individuals are identified by their name, so we identify a business primarily by its name.

The name plays a very significant part in the way the law protects a brand. Even if a business has many other symbols, like Coca-Cola with its distinctive bottle shape, the name is nevertheless a critical component of its identity. Having legal ownership of the brand name is therefore crucial. (See Chapters 2, 3, 4 and 12 for more on names.)

Values and beliefs

The values of the business's founder are paramount in establishing what a brand represents and its corporate values, as is standing for something that resonates with its customers.

In Apple's case, its name has connotations of user-friendliness, durability and quality. There are similar products on the market with good functionality, but what Apple's brand also conveys is an über-cool image. Buying Apple products has an emotional pay-off, because people you think are cool own Apple products.

If a brand can work out what it uniquely provides to its market, its marketing messages will be much more effective. You can evoke a desired response in the minds of your customers through the promise that your brand makes. Until your business can consistently deliver that, you will not have a brand.

Case study: values and beliefs of the Steve Hatt brand

In Steve Hatt's case, we could say the brand's values are to source and provide good-quality fresh fish for discerning customers who are seeking that product and prepared to pay the price.

The fact that the Steve Hatt brand has been able to consistently offer fresh, quality fish at value-for-money prices over the years is the reason the business has built trust in the minds of its target customers. They know they will get what they expect when they shop there. It eliminates the risk of the unknown.

If the business were unreliable and sometimes offered fresh fish, and other times sold fish of dubious quality, it could not hope to be associated in its customers' minds with the ability to reliably offer top-quality fresh fish. And if a change of management caused the offering to become erratic, the business would gradually lose its reputation. As a result, the pulling power of the brand would drop off and could even die if it were mismanaged over a period of time.

Sometimes, it can take just one serious event to completely destroy a reputation, especially when it is the last straw, coming at a time when the brand is already weakened as happened with Pan Am, explained by Matt Haig in *Brand Failures* (Kogan Page, 2003).

Pan Am had been operating for more than 60 years when disaster struck in the late 1980s. A bomb went off in the cargo area of a Pan Am plane en route from London to New York, causing the plane to break in two. The crash had a devastating impact on Lockerbie in Scotland, killing 11 people on the ground as well as all those on board the plane. The nature of the tragedy tarnished Pan Am's name and it never recovered. Despite its constant promises of commitment to increasing its airline's security, the public was simply not willing to fly with Pan Am any more. After three years of flying with empty seats, in 1991 the company went bankrupt and shut down.

However, Pan Am was a much weakened brand when this disaster struck, as it had financial problems. Once you have the protection of brand status, if the business does something out of character that jars with its reputation, people are actually more likely to forgive the incident and put it down to an aberration, provided the aberration does not go to the heart of the brand's promise or undermine the bond of trust between brand and customer. This became evident, for example, when rumours surfaced and were reported in a *Guardian* article on 20 February 2012 about Apple's outsourcing to a supplier in China, which uses cheap labour and dubious employment practices. These have had little impact on the Apple brand.

Know your unique value

It's important to understand your unique value. For example, if Steve Hatt's business didn't clearly understand that it is valued for offering good-quality fresh fish, it could easily lose its hard-won reputation without even realising why.

What would happen if, in response to some customers' grumbles about fish prices, it decided to focus on slashing its prices? Some of its customers would doubtlessly be satisfied, but at the expense of the quality of the fish the business could source. As such, the business could lose its hard-gained position in a bid to satisfy some of its customers. But price-sensitive customers are not necessarily the target customers of the brand. It's the customers who value quality fresh fish and understand that fish is intrinsically expensive who need to be listened to most. As the saying goes, you can't please everyone.

Similarly, a business that is doing well, but doesn't really understand why it is succeeding and what its customers are truly valuing, gaining and appreciating by doing business with it, could lose the opportunity to build on its early successes.

So, it's important to identify your core customers and know why they are using your products or services. You can then focus on satisfying their needs and get feedback on how they perceive the business.

Legal definition of a brand

According to *The New Strategic Brand Management* (Kogan Page, 2008) by J.N. Kapferer, the internationally agreed legal definition of a brand is '*a sign or set of signs certifying the origin of a product or service and differentiating it from the competition*'.

The brand name is often the primary way in which consumers identify products and services and is the 'sign' that you would expect customers to use in order to distinguish your goods and services from those of competitors.

However, there are other 'signs' that we traditionally associate with brands.

For example, logos and other visual branding help customers identify brands; examples are the Apple logo, Coca-Cola bottle shape and the Nike 'swoosh'. (See Chapter 5 for more on visual branding.)

As we know, one of the hottest points of disagreement between brand experts is the definition of a brand. The classical definition is: *'a brand is a set of mental associations, held by the consumer, which add to the perceived value of a product or service'*.

Nowadays, there are two broad camps among brand management professionals. One places a stronger emphasis on the relationship that customers have with the brand, as the dominant element of the definition, while the other emphasises the monetary value created by the brand. However, both elements are significant to the two camps.

Most importantly, the brand is how you create attachment, loyalty and willingness to buy your products and services over and over again. How your brand evokes this willingness could be due to beliefs of superiority and emotions that are activated by the brand.

In this chapter, I've explained how achieving brand status is about being known for something, and running an effective business. Throughout this book, I will use the example of a fictitious business, The Time Management Company (which, for brevity's sake, I'll refer to as TTMC), to illustrate the key points in each chapter.

A fictitious business: The Time Management Company

The Time Management Company was founded by Gavin Brown. TTMC has been established for two years and employs one permanent employee – an administrative assistant – as well as seven freelance staff who assist with content creation, social media, and web matters.

It has just appointed its second employee, Caspar Johnson, who used to assist Gavin in delivering consultancy services on a freelance basis. However, due to the growing demand for Gavin's services and the fact that Caspar was sometimes engaged on other projects when Gavin needed him, Gavin has decided to offer Caspar permanent employment as a member of his staff.

The company aims to push forward with expansion plans: it intends to license its methodology to consultants operating overseas and to introduce a number of products. Recently, it has developed an innovative desk accessory and Gavin wants to protect the IP rights in this.

The company also has growth plans and wants to put its affairs in order so as to be 'investment-ready' in case it needs to secure funding in the near future. Gavin plans to have a new website developed as the business has long outgrown its existing website, which was developed by a member of Gavin's freelance team two years ago when he set up the business.

Developing a brand is going to be an important part of the company's plans, so the first point for Gavin to consider is the suitability of its current name.

Conclusion

Our example company, TTMC, would benefit from having an in-depth conversation with a brand lawyer. By explaining its overall business plan and objectives to a lawyer, TTMC can find out the significant issues it should be addressing, such as the deficiency in its name, which we'll look at in the next chapter.

Chapter 1: Key take-home messages

- A brand is about creating a good business that's reliable and known for delivering on a specific promise.

- Every brand has its own distinct 'identity' and 'promise'.

- Everything you do, or don't do, contributes to creating the brand.

- You do not have to be big to have a brand.

- A brand is not a logo or design feature – substance is more important than surface imagery.

- A brand is identified primarily through its name.

- Understanding your unique value is core to the survival of a brand.

Chapter 2

Seven crucial points to know about trade marks and brands

'Names are everything' Oscar Wilde

In Chapter 1 we saw that trade marks are 'signs' or symbols that designate the origin of products or services. Other signs that businesses commonly use are names, logos and taglines. This chapter introduces concepts you need to know, to understand Chapters 4 and 12 on trade marks.

Your name is what you use to answer the phone, to promote and advertise your business and it's what your customers use to recommend your product or service. You build up goodwill in the name through using it. It makes sense, therefore, to own the rights in it by registering the name as a trade mark as a priority. Once registered, the rights in the name may be transferred just like any physical property.

Choosing the right name

The choice of name is important from a legal perspective. The more distinctive your name, the easier and more affordable it will be to take action against anyone who piggybacks off your success.

While lawyers generally don't pick names, leaving this to be done by marketers or business owners, it doesn't mean that the choice of name is not a legal matter. It is.

Names are to branding what land is to property development. Before you proceeded to build on a plot of land or develop a property, you would need to have various checks undertaken by lawyers. Likewise, you need a brand lawyer to advise on whether your proposed name is one you can legally own and if it's capable of achieving your ambitions for your business. Not all names are eligible for trade mark registration.

Names are not protected by copyright

Names and taglines are not copyright works and can only be protected through trade marks. Copyright is explained in Chapter 5.

The decision not to give names the benefit of copyright protection was made in 1982, in a case where Exxon Corp unsuccessfully applied to stop Exxon Insurance Consultants calling themselves Exxon, arguing that it had copyright in the name because it had spent substantial amounts of money in developing the name. The court disagreed, stating it was not possible to have copyright in a name.

The reason given was that a name is too brief to attract copyright. Regardless of how much investment is put into the creation of a name, and no matter how clever the name, from a policy point of view the court decided to keep names out of copyright and to use trade marks to determine ownership rights in names.

Descriptive trade marks are not allowed

Let's return to our example company, TTMC, introduced at the end of Chapter 1. Gavin Brown, the owner, has to come up with a more suitable brand name as part of his plans to expand the business, because 'The Time Management Company' is too descriptive a name to function as a trade mark. Gavin now understands why the choice of name is so important and that a name has to work on a number of different levels. It must:

■ attract customers; and

■ be unique and distinctive enough to register as a trade mark; and

■ **be memorable so consumers remember your business.**

When Gavin founded the company two years ago, he chose the name 'The Time Management Company' because of its marketing effectiveness. It informs consumers what the business does. However, the UK Trade Marks Act 1994 states that a mark may not be registered as a trade mark if it consists 'exclusively of signs or indications which may serve to designate the kind, value, quantity or purpose of goods or services'. Other countries' laws have similar provisions, which prevent descriptive names functioning as trade marks.

The topic of descriptiveness is a large one in trade mark law, and is discussed in Chapter 12 in more depth when we look at trade mark registration. Also, as descriptive names are used on the Internet we'll cover descriptive names in Chapters 4 and 16 too.

In addition to the above descriptive restriction, there are six key points to take into account in order to understand how trade marks operate.

1. Similar trade mark names are a problem

An important objective of trade marks is to avoid customer confusion about the source or origin of goods and services. This means if you wanted to choose a name that was already registered, it wouldn't be enough simply to make slight adjustments to the name (such as in the spelling) in order to avoid clashing with an existing registration.

If your proposed trade mark is similar to someone else's registered trade mark, it could infringe on their rights (see Chapter 15). It's a different situation, though, when it comes to choosing a domain or company name. If you find that your first choice is taken, you can usually register a similar one by tweaking the name slightly, or adding inconsequential words to it. So, if you wanted to register Galaxy.com for your confectionery business, but found the name was already taken, you could register Galaxychoc.com and secure this domain. But, with trade marks, if another confectionery business has already registered the name, you will have to find another name, and you'd be treading on dangerous ground if you included the word Galaxy at all in your name. That's why a trade mark is the way to secure rights over a name.

The broad scope of protection of trade marks looks at the issue from the customer's point of view. Let's say I've enjoyed a bar of chocolate called Galaxy and want to buy another one later. I might be confused if I find chocolate bars from other chocolate producers bearing names like Galixy, Galax or Galyx. This could result in my buying the wrong chocolate bar. The taste would be disappointing because it would be different from the one I've bought previously and was hoping to buy again.

Without the legal protection of trade marks, consumers cannot rely on finding products and services they've liked in the past and want to use again.

Generally, it's not a clear-cut case whether or not two marks are similar. It's largely dependent on whether other trade mark owners object to a mark. If they think your name is similar, you will have to justify your position and, ultimately, a court will decide the issue.

Case study: Ballon d'Or

The trade mark owner Ballon d'Or is seeking to stop Golden Balls Ltd from using the Golden Balls mark on the grounds that it is too similar to its own.

Gus and Inez Bodur had registered trade marks in the name Golden Balls in the UK, EU and other countries back in 2001 and 2002.

Their problems began when they licensed use of their name to Endemol UK plc for a TV game show. They were promptly challenged by the French firm Intra Presse, organisers of the Ballon d'Or European Footballer of the Year award. Intra Presse argued that the name Golden Balls was an infringement of their award as it was a translation of Ballon d'Or (literally, ball of gold). They asked that Golden Balls Ltd transfer their existing rights to them, on the basis that there was potential confusion between the two marks.

Although Gus and Inez were successful initially, the case is currently under appeal. As well as being an extreme example of how dissimilar names can be argued to be too similar under trade mark law, the case also shows how you can exist quite peacefully until your business moves to the next level. If you are unlucky enough to be challenged by a wealthy opponent with deep pockets, then no matter how unreasonable their case may be, you have a problem simply because they challenge your mark. You either have to respond and spend money you may not have, or give in. In either event, you will incur costs.

2. Company and domain registrations are not enough

Owning a company or domain name does not automatically give you the right to prevent others from using a similar name. Even if you have registered the .com of the name or limited company, you will still need to check the trade mark registers first.

You may well be able to use the company or domain name you've registered, provided you don't use it in competition with an existing business that has trade mark rights in the name. It depends on the business activity you want to use it for as to whether you will have a legal problem.

If your use would cause confusion with an existing business, then you would be open to challenge by a trade mark owner with rights over a similar name. The domain name may be recoverable from you too (see Chapter 16).

The single biggest reason why new businesses get caught out and need to rebrand is because they don't know they have to check the trade mark registers before using a name.

3. There's a difference between registered and unregistered trade marks

It's a popular misconception in the UK that mere use of a mark entitles the user to claim trade mark rights in it. This is not true. Another party may have better rights to the name, for instance if they have registered it as a trade mark.

Trade mark registration is how you secure rights in a name that you want to build your brand on. The name embodies the goodwill that your business generates.

However, it's not necessary to register a trade mark in order to use a name and, provided you are not infringing on somebody else's rights, you may claim a name by adding the letters ™ next to it, to indicate you are using it in a trade mark sense. But there are serious downsides to not registering a name. For a start, unbeknown to you someone else may have a registration which prevents your using the name. And someone else might begin to use the same name or register it first, and you may not be able to do anything about it.

Case study: Kalaxia

A design student had won many awards for a product he designed during his Master's degree. These awards generated quite a buzz about the name of his product. (I've called it Kalaxia to conceal the identity of the parties.) He intended to set up a business using that name once he completed his studies.

Soon afterwards, he noticed that a business offering a competing product to the one he developed had registered the name as a trade mark, beating him to it.

Even though the student had received extensive press coverage and recognition for his innovative Kalaxia product, he had not used the name to sell goods or services, so he could not validly object to the competitor's registration.

His competitor may well have acted unethically in 'stealing' the Kalaxia name (and with it the good associations that the press coverage and awards had given it), but the student was powerless to object. Even if he could have challenged the competitor, he certainly did not have the financial resources to start his business life by engaging in legal action.

The moral is clear: if you have a name you are keen on and want to use as your brand (business) name, then it's important to register it as a trade mark immediately in order to secure your rights in it.

However, if you have been using a name for a long time, you may have built up sufficient rights in it to be able to stop another party using the same name, on the grounds that they are 'passing off' their business as yours. Bear in mind, though, that it costs time and money to take action in these situations and you face all the uncertainties of litigation.

If you lose the chance to own a name, you've not only lost the name but also wasted time and resources developing an identity around a name you cannot own.

If you don't have a registered trade mark, then a claim of 'passing off' (explained in Chapter 15) is the only avenue open to you for objecting to someone else's use of a similar name.

4. Trade marks are territorial

Trade marks are registered on a country-by-country basis. So, if you register a trade mark with the UK Intellectual Property Office, it will give you the rights to use your mark in the UK. But if someone based in another country (such as the US) used the same mark, your UK mark does not give you the right to stop them. (More about this in Chapter 12.)

5. Trade marks comprise certain categories of goods or services

Names can be shared by more than one business, provided the businesses are not in competition with each other. The reason for this is that trade marks are registered against classifications, and you are permitted to use the trade mark for those predefined categories of business.

There are 45 classes in all. The overriding issue is that names must not cause confusion to consumers looking to buy products and services. A business engaged in mining is therefore unlikely to be confused with a clothing business with the same name.

It's possible, then, for the same name to be a registered trade mark of several different businesses. The question of whether or not it causes confusion is to look at the issue from the consumer's point of view. Would the consumer assume that the goods or services came from the same source? If not, then different trade mark owners may share the same name. For example, Polo is a registered trade mark belonging to three businesses operating in different sectors – cars, confectionery and clothes.

The 45 classes of trade mark categories are based on an internationally agreed system, known as the 'Nice Classification'. The Nice system, which is used in more than 140 countries, groups together broadly similar goods or services into categories. This helps the registry to carry out efficient searches of the register. Classes 1–34 relate to goods, while classes 35–45 cover services.

The World Intellectual Property Office (WIPO) administers the Nice Classifications and aims to revise them every three to five years by removing any anomalies and inconsistencies that have been found. New entries are added in order to improve the classifications. An updated tenth edition of the list was published for 2012 and is now in use by the UK Trade Mark Registry.

6. Famous marks are an exception to the classification rule

A famous or well-known mark may enjoy broader protection than an ordinary mark, in view of its widespread reputation or recognition. Such marks are not subject to the classification restriction.

Most industrialised countries afford broad protection to owners of well-known trade marks. What this means is that if you picked a famous brand name such as Martini or Coca-Cola as your brand name, then Martini or Coca-Cola could stop you from using their name even if you were intending to run a business in a completely different area of industry.

A well-known mark enjoys the same protection as if it had been registered in each of the 45 classes. However, beyond household names the issue is not always straightforward. A mark may be well known in one country but not in another and it depends on whether the public in the given territory is familiar with the mark.

An example of a case where a well-known mark failed to stop another business using its name is the drinks company V&S Vin & Sprit, which owns the Absolut Vodka brand. It issued proceedings against Virgin's Absolute Radio for trade mark infringement and passing off on the basis that there was a risk of confusion with its brand. Absolute Radio was registered as a trade mark in 2003, and Absolut was aiming to have the trade mark revoked.

After 18 months of wrangling, a confidential settlement ensued whereby Absolute Radio was able to continue using the name.

Therefore, avoid using the name of a mark that is well known in the country in which you intend using it. Otherwise you could be required to rebrand even if you have secured trade mark, domain or company registrations.

There have been applications to register Twitter for wine, beer and other alcoholic drinks, as well as attempts at other categories. The objection to such applications is that, by using the sign, the applicant is taking unfair advantage of the mark's fame and its use could have a detrimental impact on the well-known trade mark.

Conclusion

It's important to understand the key principles about trade marks before choosing a brand name as there are a number of considerations to take into account. Before Gavin, our example business owner, chooses a name for his company, he will want to understand these issues a little better, and we'll look at brand-naming strategy in the next chapter.

Chapter 2: Key take-home messages

■ The most important asset to protect is your name.

■ Choose a distinctive name so you can register it as a trade mark.

■ Names and taglines are not protected by copyright.

■ Securing a domain name or limited company won't give you the automatic right to use the name – it depends on the business you want to use it for as to whether you may use the name.

■ Avoid using well-known names in your brand name.

Chapter 3

Planning your naming and brand strategy

'A product can be quickly outdated, but a successful brand is timeless'
Stephen King

Once you have decided on a name for your business, the first step is to have the name assessed by a lawyer. If you get the green light, you can then buy a domain name and register a trade mark at the same time.

Although brand names raise many legal issues, small businesses don't enjoy the same access to lawyers as large companies do. A common mistake is to pick a name, see if the desired domain is available, have designers produce a logo and identity and then consult a lawyer to protect the name once all the branding work has been carried out.

When is rebranding desirable?

One of the commonest reasons for rebranding is when a business wants to expand and its existing name is too descriptive to trade mark, as is the case with our example company, The Time Management Company.

There are countless instances of businesses that have rebranded for this reason. Business Network International became BNI; Keystone Law, a virtual law firm, was originally known as Lawyers Direct; British Telecommunications plc became BT; and the Hong Kong and Shanghai Banking Corporation became HSBC.

You only need look at Interbrand's Top 100 brands to see that every company in the list either has a distinctive name, or uses initials (invariably, initials are used because the company started out with a descriptive name that was not eligible for use as a trade mark).

Otherwise, as long as there is nothing fundamentally wrong with your brand name, why change it? Changing the name will not guarantee success. Unless there are compelling reasons to do so, rebranding risks undermining previous marketing efforts.

If you do decide to rebrand, consider if there might be unexpected consequences by taking the following steps.

Consult your customers first

Existing customers are often averse to name or logo changes they perceive to be unnecessary. When Gap decided to redesign its logo, it was unprepared for the backlash and the extreme displeasure its new logo evoked. More than 2,000 comments were posted on the company's Facebook page, most of them demanding the return of the traditional logo. The online outcry led to Gap scrapping the new logo, saying 'the company's customers always come first'.

Check the translation

Certain names are ill-advised because they have unfortunate – and sometimes hilarious – connotations. Names such as the Pocari Sweat health drink and names that don't translate effectively into other languages are unhelpful.

For example, beer maker Coors discovered that its slogan, 'Turn it loose', translated into Spanish as 'Suffer from diarrhoea'. Chevrolet launched its Chevy Nova car in Spain under the same name, which translates as 'Does not go'. American Airlines advertised the luxurious aspect of flying business class to its Mexican customers by focusing on the leather seats, using the slogan 'Fly in Leather', which translates as 'Vuelo en Cuero' in Spanish. The Spanish dictionary neglected to inform them that the phrase 'en cuero' is a slang term for 'in the nude'. Unsurprisingly, there was little demand for mile-high naturism among Mexico's business flyers.

Other reasons to rebrand

Sometimes a company is forced into rebranding because its name infringes on the rights of others (as we'll see in Chapter 15). If this happens to you, see if you can negotiate extra time so you have some breathing space to choose another name.

Speak Etc.

Robyn Hatcher of Speak Etc. had been running her coaching and consulting business under the name Speakeasy for almost 15 years before she was threatened with a trade mark infringement lawsuit, according to a blog post by Kelly Watson in Forbes.com.

Hatcher reportedly said: 'As a first-time entrepreneur I jumped into the business naively. My research consisted of Googling the name and seeing what came up in the top searches. What came up were several companies that were completely different, so I considered myself safe'.

Hatcher received an email threatening litigation if she didn't take down her website and change her business name.

Doing a Ratner

Another situation where you would change your name is if there has been a reputation-damaging incident, such as the Ratners experience.

The famous jewellery mogul Gerald Ratner referred to the products his business was selling as 'crap' during a speech at the Institute of Directors in 1991, as Rob Brown explains in his book *How to Build Your Reputation* (Ecademy Press, 2007):

Although the shops were widely regarded as tacky, the wares were extremely popular with the public. However, during his speech Gerald Ratner said: 'We also do cut-glass sherry decanters complete with six glasses on a silver-plated tray that your butler can serve you drinks on, all for £4.95. People say, "How can you sell this for such a low price?" I say, because it's total crap'. He compounded this by going on to remark that some of the earrings were 'cheaper than an M&S prawn sandwich but probably wouldn't last as long'.

An estimated £500m was wiped from the value of the company. The company rebranded but business never recovered from this setback and the Ratner name was eventually dropped in favour of Signet.

Timing your rebrand

If you decide you need to rebrand, the best time to choose a better name is once the business concept is proven and you know the business is clearly going to be viable. It's not a good idea to continue with a descriptive name beyond that point as doing so will hold your business back in the long run.

Consumers choose products and services by name. It's therefore important to build up recognition in your name as early as possible, otherwise your business may miss out on the potential to increase revenue and the goodwill generated will be lost.

How important is the brand to your business?

As our example company, TTMC, is intending to build a business to sell, it should consider whether the brand is likely to be an important component of such a sale. Who might buy the business?

For some types of business the brand will be key. For others, the brand will have little significance because the potential buyer may only be interested to buy the business for its operational achievements, its technology, or some other desirable element.

Examples of businesses where the brand is important are Zumba Fitness and the Anywayup Cup. In both cases the name has become synonymous with how people recognise the concept or product.

An example of a business that would not be reliant on its name is MES International. Its core activity consists of selling consumables for the quarrying and mining industry to a small client base. If the business were sold, its activities could still be continued, supplying the same customer base while operating under a different name. Know-how and customer relationships are likely to be the greatest assets in a business such as this.

Where the brand is an integral component of the business, the choice of name is very important, as is owning the rights in it. As you can't be certain early on whether the brand will become a valuable asset, it's worth assuming that the brand will matter, if you are planning to sell the business in the near future.

Taglines

Taglines, slogans and catchphrases are sometimes used as part of a company's unique selling point (USP). Although some people argue that the concept of USP is now outdated, taglines do have a place in communicating a brand's values.

As we saw earlier, names can only be protected through trade marks, not copyright. Similarly, taglines are unlikely to be copyright works, although it is unclear how long a tagline would need to be in order to attract copyright protection in its own right.

Where a business has been using a descriptive name, but is now rebranding, it may make sense to retain the descriptive element as its tagline, either on its own, or combined with other wording that explains the company's values or USP. Therefore, our example company, TTMC, might consider incorporating Time Management Company in a tagline, possibly as part of a slogan.

Trade-marking taglines

It may be possible to register a slogan or tagline as a trade mark, depending on whether the particular tagline is descriptive. TTMC would not be able to register its tagline as a trade mark without adding something else to Time Management Company to create a distinctive slogan.

Some well-known taglines that are registered trade marks include John Lewis's 'Never knowingly undersold', Tesco's 'Every little helps' and Nike's 'Just do it'.

There are a limited number of messages that can encapsulate how competing brands differ from one another. For example, quality and price are going to be strong contenders for any supermarket food brand. Finding a clever way to communicate your message, and using it in a tagline that can be trade-marked, will prevent others from using the same wording for their messages.

An Azrights tagline 'Easy legal not legalese', was registered without difficulty in 2010 and is an example of the type of message that many law firms might want to communicate about themselves. Nobody has a monopoly on claiming that they communicate in plain English, so there's a real value in communicating a message in a distinctive and evocative way so that your competitors cannot freely copy it.

Approaches to branding

When choosing a name, be clear about your objectives so that your name reflects what your business is aiming to achieve.

To return to our example company, Gavin Brown, founder of TTMC, has written a book describing his methodology, and this forms a central component of the business. The book is called *How To Manage Information Overload*. He wonders whether he could use the book's title or his own name as the brand name for his business. Another possible candidate for the name is the abbreviation TTMC.

Firstly, the title of the book would not be suitable as a brand name because it too is descriptive. And his own name, Gavin Brown, is too common a name to function as a trade mark. But TTMC is a possibility, and it's a good idea for him come up with a shortlist of names for possible trade mark registration.

Certain industries, such as fashion or design, frequently use the business founder's name as the brand name. Companies like Disney, Dell, and Ford all bear their founders' names. This is perfectly acceptable, providing your name is suitable and distinctive enough. But a common name cannot be protected.

Types of brand names

Broadly speaking, there are three types of brand name.

1. Proper marks are words that use the business owner's own name or a made-up name for the brand. Well-known names that fall into this category include Disney, Coca-Cola, Paul Smith, Vivienne Westwood, Microsoft, eBay and Starbucks. Designers, photographers and other creative types tend to use their own name as a trade mark.

Paul Smith is an example of a common name that would not usually be eligible for trade mark protection, but gained trade mark status for the designer because the name became well known. Occasionally, a common name like Paul Smith, or a descriptive name like Philadelphia cheese, acquire 'distinctiveness' and therefore attains trade mark status. (More about trade mark registration in Chapter 12.)

2. Common marks are names using real words whose meaning bears no relation to the goods or services of the brand. Examples are Apple, Shell, Amazon, Red Bull, Banana Republic, Egg, and Virgin.

3. Descriptive marks are names that describe the goods or services to which they are attached. (For detailed information on descriptive names, see Chapters 4 and 12.)

If a mark is merely suggestive of the product or service, it will fall on the right side of trade mark law and be eligible for trade mark status. Examples of names that are suggestive of their product or service include Toys "R" Us or Hotel Chocolat. These combine a descriptive term with another element to create a new common word mark. Microsoft is a made-up proper name that is suggestive of the category, and is formed by combining the first part of the word 'microcomputer' with the first part of the word 'software'.

Similarly, Azrights is a made-up proper name, which takes the term 'A-Z' and combines it with the word 'rights'.

The closer a common word mark gets to purely describing the product or service, the less likely it is to be deemed suggestive. The word mark could then fall on the wrong side of descriptive, and will not be able to function as a trade mark.

A trade mark gives a business a monopoly over its name and will often become its most valuable intellectual property asset after other assets have expired.

As long as a trade mark remains in use it may be renewed indefinitely. Kodak was first registered as a trade mark in 1888, though sadly it has recently folded, having failed to adapt to the new environment.

Characteristics of a good name

So what makes a good brand name? A descriptive name that is suggestive of a product or service, but doesn't actually describe it, such as Hotel Chocolat, is an effective name. It's the ideal to aim for if you want your name to have marketing appeal.

What determines whether a name is a good one will depend on the markets in which you trade. Names should also be easy to pronounce and spell, and be unique to you, and nowhere is this more important than when establishing an online presence.

Be aware that names could limit or restrict you later if you were to expand into other areas. 'Pandora Soup Cafe' would find it more difficult to start selling salads or sandwich products, as well as soup, than if it simply called itself Pandora.

On the other hand, Carphone Warehouse is an example of a brand that has managed to transcend a limiting name. But, rather than using this as an example in favour of using a limiting name, it's best to regard it as an exception to the rule, and not point to it as a reason to justify a limiting name.

While made-up names are ideal in trade mark terms, because they are likely to be unique, they may not be so appealing from a marketing perspective because consumers won't know what the business does when they hear its name. It may be better only to opt for a completely made-up name if your business is going to emulate the success of Google or Twitter. The massive adoption of the business model is what helps these brands to have a highly recognised mark, despite being made-up names.

Naming strategy and your business plan

It helps to have your business plan in mind when deciding on your naming strategy. If you are intending to introduce products and services in the future, it's never too soon to think about how you will name them.

> TTMC has plans to introduce software, courses on time management, a membership site, coaching, T-shirts, CDs, starter packs, and a host of other products and services. So, an early question for the business is how to brand everything.

Taking time to consider your naming strategy in advance makes it easier to pick names and to reach decisions as you develop products and services. It also saves time because as your business grows and adds further products and services, or opens related businesses, it'll be far easier to know what to do and how to avoid expensive mistakes.

So, what are the options and considerations?

- **Is your brand name portable? As part of your naming strategy, consider how portable your primary brand name would be for other products and services that you might offer in future. That is, if your intention is to use the primary brand name across your products and services.**

- **Check how other brands have tackled the issues. There's some debate over the best branding strategy to adopt when selling multiple products. Being aware of the issues and seeing how some**

> household brands have tackled these questions is a good way to
> decide on your own strategy.
>
> ■ **Decide on your focus. The main question is whether to focus on
> an umbrella brand and promote all products under this brand
> name, or whether to create multiple brands for each new product
> that's launched. The umbrella brand approach is known as 'house
> branding' while a multiple brand strategy is termed 'house of
> brands'.**

Looking at how big established companies handle their branding is a good way to assess the different approaches to branding in action. There is no 'right' way to name products and services. A lot depends on your market and business plan objectives.

House of brands v. house brand

Procter & Gamble is an example of a 'house of brands' approach to branding. This is where a business might have many brands, each one being a stand-alone name.

People are often surprised to learn that Proctor & Gamble's products include household names such as Ariel, Tide, Wella, Head & Shoulders, and Olay. Procter & Gamble's business name is not as well known as the names of many of its products.

If Procter & Gamble were to start trading under a different business name, the effect on its products would be minimal and the majority of consumers would be unlikely to even notice. When buying Head & Shoulders shampoo, customers do not choose it because it is made by Procter & Gamble. They buy it because they have trust in the Head & Shoulders brand.

The other approach to branding, the 'house brand', is where the company focuses on one main brand, which runs through all its subsequent product names. An example is Virgin, where the same name is used across a number of different businesses, with the addition of descriptors such as Virgin Atlantic, Virgin Hotels, Virgin Media, Virgin Records, and so on.

One of the considerations in deciding whether to use a 'house of brands' or a 'house brand' approach is cost; the other is the nature of your products and services.

Google's naming strategy

Google's approach to branding received much attention after its decision to name its new social media site 'Google+'. Alongside the introduction of Google+, two of its existing products are undergoing a rebrand while the long-standing products Picasa and Blogger are being retired. Picasa becomes 'Google Photos' while Blogger becomes 'Google Blogs'.

So Google changed its branding strategy to focus on launching its new products under the Google brand name, using Google News, Google Translate, Google Chrome, and so on. One of the primary questions raised by this move to brand all products under the same name is whether these products will benefit by association, or whether the Google brand will suffer.

Over the years, Google has been a highly rated brand, one that is trusted and respected. So, any new products would, in theory, benefit from using its name. However, the decision to brand its social media site under the Google brand name has come under scrutiny.

'Google' as a name is associated with a search engine rather than a social network. When you hear the name 'Google', you don't think of 'social'. By creating a variety of different products under the same brand name, one risk is that the main brand will become diluted. The reason why Google as a brand name is powerful is because the brand is immediately associated with its main service as a search engine. With its new naming strategy, there is the danger that the brand is trying to cover too many products and services.

In branding, it's important for a product to have a specific connotation that's related to the brand, to establish a foothold within the market.

Benefits of 'house brands'

The benefit of the 'house brand' approach is that it's financially more economic. By taking one strong brand, and ploughing all your brand meaning into it, while differentiating each product with descriptors instead of brand names, you avoid the need for legal clearance and trade mark registration each time you release a new product.

When you have one main brand, resources can be focused on creating and building this brand, rather than having to spread them by creating several different brands, and then trade-marking these. This method is more cost-effective.

By creating a strong main brand, any new product immediately benefits from its association with the main brand.

However, one danger in having all of a company's services and products marketed under one brand name is the risk of the brand as a whole being damaged if one of the products develops a bad reputation. This is what happened to Unilever, as we'll see below.

Benefits of 'house of brands'

Procter & Gamble's well-known brands such as Gillette, Olay, and Duracell have little association with the company itself. They are created, marketed and branded individually, and each brand stands on its own feet.

Many people do not even realise that certain products are under common ownership. In this example, Procter & Gamble's brand name does not add any extra credibility to a product. However, Procter & Gamble still has an extremely successful business, having established many different, well-respected brands.

One advantage of this 'umbrella' approach to branding is that it enables a number of different products to be created. Each new product can be marketed separately and aimed at different audiences without diluting the main company's brand. Each product is then able to establish itself on its own grounds, without being constrained by assumptions associated with the main brand.

Each brand stands for completely different values and represents unrelated products, from snacks to personal grooming. With such a range and variety of products, it would be impossible to brand them all under the same umbrella brand name, and the 'house of brands' method is the most appropriate for this business model.

Unilever's mistake

Unilever is an interesting company to look at in terms of brand architecture. Like Procter & Gamble, Unilever started off using the 'house of brands' approach, and all its products stood alone, being completely separate from Unilever itself. However, because of the lack of recognition of the main Unilever brand, the company decided to take a 'house brand' approach and endorse all its products with a 'U' logo. But this transition backfired, after it launched an ad for Dove cosmetics that campaigned for 'real beauty'. After the launch, there was much debate concerning the different ideals promoted by Dove compared to those promoted by its Lynx ads, which have a reputation for being sexist.

This conflict in ideology arising from having two products under the same brand was heavily criticised. The negative outcome stemmed from the connection created between previously seemingly unconnected products. As a result, Unilever's desire for the main brand to become more involved in the marketing of its products was unsustainable.

The Unilever example demonstrates how, in a 'house brand' situation, it's important for all the products and services to represent the same essential values. If this is not feasible, then using the Procter & Gamble 'house of brands' approach would be more appropriate.

Hybrid approach

Apple employs a tactic that lies somewhere in between the 'house brand' and the 'house of brands' – along the lines of the one Unilever attempted to employ by endorsing all its products with a 'U' logo. This approach is called the 'house blend'.

Apple launches its new products and services under new names, using the lower-case 'i' to distinguish its products while still retaining the emphasis on the main Apple brand.

Although Apple's approach is to create a new name for each new product, it still does not completely use the 'house of brands' approach. All the products and services are endorsed and given credibility by the overriding Apple brand. What Apple has done is build two brand levels – the Apple brand itself and the sub-brands such as 'iPod' 'Macbook', 'iPad', and so on. This way, each product and service has its own separate brand while the Apple brand name is still strongly associated with each service or product it creates.

Apple has an iconic brand, which is 'about imagination, design and innovation'. So this emotional component is brought to each of its products. But, by creating separate sub-brands, Apple has been able to expand into the music business as well as consumer electronics and computer software without diluting its brand image.

Conclusion

Looking at the different approaches to branding taken by the companies highlighted in this chapter, it is evident that there is no single way to approach branding. Nor is there any set way to go about choosing a good name.

The 'house brand' approach would be far better for businesses that do not want to devote the financial resources required to promoting several different brands. In Gavin's company, where all the products are within similar categories and aimed at the same markets while promoting similar values, the 'house brand' approach makes more sense.

Chapter 3: Key take-home messages

■ Get a lawyer to check out your business name before producing a logo or registering a domain name – it will save you time and money in the long run.

■ Don't rebrand unless there are compelling reasons to do – it could undermine previous marketing efforts.

■ The best time to rebrand is when your business concept is proven.

■ If you need to change a descriptive brand name, consider incorporating the descriptive element in the tagline or slogan so you don't lose out on previous marketing expenditure.

■ Choose a brand name that's easy to pronounce and spell, and that's unique to you.

Chapter 4

Understanding the role of keywords, domain names and SEO in online branding

'Without deviation from the norm, progress is not possible' Frank Zappa

The Internet is changing fast, so it's important to keep abreast of developments when it comes to branding best practice. What may have been the right way to name a business a few years ago may no longer be valid today. In particular, social media is adding to the pace of change, and so the need to stand out from the competition is more important than ever in the crowded Internet landscape.

As with any branding, the choice of name is important when it comes to setting up online. The name needs to be effective from a marketing perspective and attract customers. It also has to be unique, memorable and distinctive enough to stand out online, as well as suitable for registering as a trade mark to protect your business and secure its assets.

Remember that once your business is successful, others tend to imitate you. By then it may be too late to rebrand if you haven't chosen a unique identity that prevents competitors setting up in your space by using similar names.

The early days of the Internet

In the early days of the Internet, the web was like a small village with perhaps one or two of each type of business: a toy shop, a grocery store, a bookshop, a hotel, and so on. It was therefore common for businesses to call themselves by descriptive names, and to use domain names like toys.com, books.com, pets.com, hotels.com, etc.

Determining whether a name is descriptive or not depends on the context in which it is used. For instance, if you owned a flower shop and called your business 'Flowers', you would be using a name that describes the goods or services of the business, and such a name cannot function as a trade mark. But if your shop sold products that had nothing to do with flowers, chocolates say, then Flowers could be a perfectly acceptable name from a trade mark point of view.

As more and more businesses set up on the Internet, the descriptive, 'small village' approach to naming becomes more inappropriate. But it's a common misconception that using a descriptive name is the way to go. Descriptive names continue to have a strong appeal, and many businesses who set up online choose to go down this route. But, with millions of sites vying for attention on the Internet, it's questionable whether this is a sensible approach.

Hotels.com

Hotels.com is an example of a business that was founded in the early days of the Internet when it was fashionable to use generic descriptive names as a brand name.

The company put forward evidence to persuade the United States Patent and Trademark Office (USPTO) that its brand had acquired distinctiveness during the 20 years it had been in business. (The fact that Hotels.com actually went to this expense is a testament to the importance of trade marks to established businesses.)

After carrying out a nationwide survey of consumers, the company found that consumers regarded Hotels.com as a brand name. Nevertheless, the USPTO held that the mark was generic, and Hotels.com lost the case.

In opting for a descriptive name, Hotels.com left itself vulnerable. Apart from not being able to trade-mark the name, the downside to using a purely descriptive name is that there is little you can do in practical terms when a competitor sets up with a similar name. Although on the Internet there may be only one Hotels.com in the physical world dozens of hotels could call themselves Hotels.com, and divert goodwill away from the original Hotels.com.

Online approach to naming

You may see many other sites using keyword-rich names, but don't necessarily be tempted to assume you should follow suit without further consideration of the issues. The growth of social media adds to the level of 'noise' online, so a descriptive name will make you less memorable.

In the short term, descriptive names help you to communicate what your business is about. People will immediately know that a business with the name Books4Less is about books and low prices. On the other hand, people won't automatically realise that a company with the name Amazon sells books, or that it aims to give people a good price. But once they've shopped at Amazon, its singular name means it is more likely to be etched in their memory than a non-distinctive name like Books4Less.

Over time, the generic name of Books4Less will be easily confused with the many similar keyword-rich domain names in use by competitors. Inevitably, Books4Less will lose valuable business because it chose a descriptive domain name. It's no coincidence that many successful online businesses, such as Google, eBay, Twitter, and Pinterest, have distinctive names. So, try to emulate the successful Internet businesses by choosing a distinctive brand name.

Interestingly, Google started out as BackRub, Distilled was initially Wandd, while eBay began life as AuctionWeb. So, TTMC is in good company in rebranding in the early stages in order to have a more distinctive name.

As Al and Laura Ries put it in their excellent book *The 11 Immutable Laws of Internet Branding* (Harper Collins, 2001):

How can we be so sure that proper names will prevail over common names as brand names on the Internet? The only proof is a hundred years of history. In the past century, how many common names have become successful brands? Very, very few.

These days, as with any brand name, distinctive names work much more effectively on the Internet. The descriptive-named businesses of the early Internet days came and went. Despite enjoying serious venture capital backing, they have faded into oblivion. All they have left behind are valuable domain names that may have changed hands several times by now, and are principally valuable for search purposes. For example, books. com redirects to Barnes & Noble, bringing extra traffic to that site.

Reduced value of the brand

If you are not able to legally 'own' your brand name through trade mark registration, the value of your brand will inevitably be reduced. There are many other downsides. As we've seen, customers could be confused if someone else started using a similar name. For example, if a competitor to our example company, The Time Management Company, set up as 'The Time Management Alliance', it would be confusing for customers. Prospective customers who were directed to The Time Management Company in their searches would not necessarily remember such fine distinctions between the names.

From a practical point of view, using a descriptive domain name for your online business renders you powerless to stop competitors stealing your market share. You are unable to prevent others registering the same name with a different suffix (e.g. '.biz', '.org', or '.info', rather than 'co.uk'). Your only recourse is likely to be to an expensive passing off action (see Chapter 15). Even then, it's highly unlikely that a judge would be willing to stop your competitor using a purely descriptive name. The Hotels.com example, above, shows how difficult it is to trade mark a generic name.

You need a *name*, not a description of your business

It's important that the name by which consumers find you on the Internet is one that's memorable, rather than one describing your business activities. A business without a name (in this sense) would be at a serious disadvantage if it needed to take action against unfair competition.

Unfortunately, many businesses discover this too late. If you have a descriptive domain name and someone else registers a similar name, it's not possible to lay claim to it, even if the name is confusingly similar to your domain name and has been specifically registered to take advantage of your reputation. But if you have a distinctive name, it's possible even to recover misspellings of your name. A few years ago, Microsoft was able to take action in a number of countries to recover domain names that incorporated misspelt versions of its name from cybersquatters. (see Chapter 16 for more information on domain disputes.)

It's true, Google rewards descriptive names

Google's search algorithm rewards descriptive names, in that the domain name is one of the factors that the search engine currently uses in determining which sites to display in response to surfers' search queries. The effects are then compounded because links to the site from other sites will often include the domain name as the link text, and it's this link text that Google uses to rank sites when searching.

Taking TTMC's domain name (timemanagementco.com) as an example, if someone entered the search term (keyword) 'time management' into Google, one of the many factors that Google's algorithm will take into account, in deciding whether to feature TTMC's website among the search results, is its domain name.

Other important considerations are:

■ the page rank – how much of an authority your site is deemed to be on the subject of time management, based on links from other sites;

■ how easy it is for the search engine to read your web pages;

■ the way your pages are structured and the platform it is built on; and

■ the keywords in the page titles and headings that your website is optimised for.

I will return to this subject of how to make your name choice, given that Google rewards descriptive names. First I will outline a few important points about how people search for information online, and how search engine optimisation methods are used by online businesses who wish to be found in response to searches by potential customers.

Keywords to Google success

Keywords are the words that people use when searching online.

Because of the way Google's system works, it's necessary to specify one original domain name for your website and then redirect any other domain names that you use to the original domain. So, if you were using ten different domain names for your website, perhaps a '.com', a '.net', as well as a 'co.uk', you would have to decide which one of them you wanted to build ranking for, and then all the other names would redirect to it (meaning the address bar would change after you've typed in the address). This is the principal domain name choice we're looking at in this chapter.

If a user searched for 'green eggs and ham', a web page with that precise text ranks higher than a page containing 'lime-coloured hen spawn & pig parts' (this example is taken from an article on the SEOmoz website at seomoz.org). Both keywords mean the same thing, but one is more precise and closer to the actual search term used by the user.

One method of finding keywords for your business is to get input from people who are potential buyers of your products and services, so you can work out the phrases they might use when searching for your type of business.

Ask yourself:

■ If my company is providing the answers, what are the questions?

■ If I have information and DVDs for sale on how to manage time, and

someone was interested in those things, what would they search for?

Common sense would tell you that keywords like 'time management'and 'information overload' are likely to figure highly. There are also a number of software tools on the web that can help you find sets of keywords, including WordTracker and Google Keyword Tool.

Understanding keywords, including how to analyse their effectiveness, where to use them, and when not to use them are all important topics both for search engine optimisation (SEO) and other online activities.

For example, when using AdWords (see Chapter 10), social media, issuing news releases, blogging, tagging, YouTube videos and monitoring your online reputation, the question that will keep coming up is 'which keywords would I target out of the many hundreds or thousands that could be relevant to my products and services?'

Knowing which keywords to target for your business is vital to building an effective online brand. So if your keyword was 'managing information', your information management business would be competing with every single information management website on the Internet. Good luck! But if you aimed to attract users searching for 'information management London', you'd narrow the field considerably.

Black hat v. white hat

If you engage a search engine optimisation (SEO) professional to improve the ranking of your web pages in search results, the approach they use is typically categorised under two camps (or hats), as described below. Make sure you use someone trustworthy (i.e. 'white hat') so you avoid the situation where your site gets lost rather than being found online. Finding good service providers is never easy, so ask around for recommendations. Take up references, and assess how long the proposed business has been established and what resources it has. Ask if the business outsources and, if so, how does it exercise quality control over its freelancers? Who are the freelancers, what work does the business outsource and how does it decide who to use?

The surest way to appear high in the search engines is to produce good content so that others link to it. There are many other techniques that can improve your prospects. Some of these are known as 'white hat' techniques, which are quite acceptable as they aim to work with the search engines. These techniques involve working within the search engine's standards and using legitimate methods so that the content has a better chance of being found.

Specialist SEO companies trying to help your site be found may accidentally cross the line of what is acceptable, even though they are aiming to avoid what are called 'black hat' techniques. Black hat SEOs mainly aim for short-term results and trick search engines and dupe them. They generate results quickly, receive their fee, and disappear. If their methods are discovered, you as owner of the site, run the risk of being penalised, which could mean you stop being found and suffer significant losses overnight. So, always use a trusted Internet professional for SEO.

Alongside constant efforts by SEOs – of both the black and white hat variety – to optimise sites for Google or other search engines in order to produce better search results for their clients, the search algorithms are continually being refined. If Google allowed third parties to manipulate search results, they would be unlikely to keep their brand promise, which is to give searchers a good user experience.

Using your chosen keywords to decide your domain name

We've seen how an important aspect of online visibility and effectiveness is to choose the correct keywords to optimise for your website. Once you've identified one or more good keywords, you can decide on your primary domain name.

Let's say you've identified that the keyword 'managing time' could bring about 27,000 potential visitors to your site each month; what are the issues to be aware of in terms of registering and using this descriptive term as a domain name 'managingtime.com'?

One obvious point to be aware of before using a descriptive domain name is whether those 27,000 potential visitors will come from within your desired geographic area. Another is whether the name will unduly narrow the services you might wish to provide. If you also want to provide leadership team-building services, is 'time management' a niche that would enable you to supply other related services?

In some lines of business, potential customers will take a pot shot and just guess a domain name to find a website that provides the products or services they are looking for. However, there is anecdotal evidence that only about 20% of surfers search this way. Even though a keyword-rich, descriptive domain name would help searchers to find you more easily in a Google search, there are some drawbacks.

Disadvantage of using descriptive domain names

Returning to the question, why not register a descriptive domain given that Google rewards descriptive names, one disadvantage is that descriptive domain names are not memorable. When a visitor finds your site and loves your products, how will they remember you, or tell their friends about your business? When they need another time management product a year later, how likely is it that they will remember the exact generic name they searched to find your site? How will you ensure they do not confuse it with a similar generic name? They might just as easily recall it as 'timemanagementskills', 'managetime' or 'timemanaging', or another combination.

This is also a concern for businesses offline, but the problem is compounded online because competitors can – and do – easily secure similar generic domain names and compete for your niche.

Another drawback is that the domain name can only be optimised for one search term out of the many that may be used. In the discussion below, about whether to opt for a keyword-rich name or a brand name, I hope it will become clearer as to how to make the right choice for your business.

Using non-SEO friendly keywords as domains

People often choose a random sentence or tagline as a keyword because they think sentences are the way to go when choosing domain names. For example, if TTMC decided to register the domain name 'amtimechallenged' simply because it liked that phrase, it would not only forego the benefits of having a distinctive and memorable domain name, it wouldn't even have a keyword-rich one. If it has already decided not to use a keyword-rich name, it would be wiser for TTMC to use its brand name instead of a random phrase.

Keyword-rich name or brand name?

From a branding point of view, it's desirable to use a domain name that matches your brand name. Using a consistent brand name and domain address avoids confusion, so only deviate from this approach for good reason, such as to secure a keyword advantage.

If you've decided to opt for a keyword-rich domain name, make sure you choose a different name for your business and not a descriptive name like 'managing time', for example. So if you were a search-engine business like Google, your choices would be to:

- **use your brand name as both your domain name and trade mark, e.g. in the case of Google, this would be google.com; or**
- **use a hybrid approach by combining your brand name with a descriptive URL (e.g. Google with a descriptive URL like searchengine.com); or**
- **give your business a descriptive name and use a descriptive URL (e.g. Search Engine and searchengine.com).**

For reasons already described, the third option is not recommended.

Drawbacks of the hybrid approach

Using a hybrid approach (that is, a brand name plus a descriptive domain name) might seem like a win-win situation, but it has its downsides.

When I initially chose Azrights as a business name, the .com domain name was unavailable. As it was important for me to have a .com address, I opted to register ip-brands.com as our main domain. It's not necessarily an approach I would recommend or use today. I have since acquired the azrights.com address, but that was only after several years of using ip-brands.com as our main URL.

An alternative approach would have been to add an additional component to the name, such as AzrightsSolicitors.com. As it is, we have had a number of people referring to us as IP Brands. To minimise the confusion, we began using azrights.co.uk as our email address, rather than ip-brands.com, which is what we used previously. So our business cards featured azrights.co.uk, as both our email and website address.

Of course, the URL redirected to ip-brands.com when people visited azrights.co.uk. So it's not possible to completely overcome the downsides of having a different name and website address. But it can be an acceptable compromise if you really want to use a descriptive domain name, provided you adopt uniform branding on your business cards. It's also important to have the right technical support so you don't lose valuable Google benefits when people enter your address, for example, azrights.co.uk instead of ip-brands.com.

Conclusion

Gavin, the owner of TTMC, should have an in-depth conversation with his brand lawyer to take account of the issues around online branding when choosing his new brand name and a domain name. Search engine optimisation is an important consideration when deciding on your online presence.

How to choose a brand name you can own

Work out your niche and describe it

↓

Choose a distinctive brand name for your business

↓

Have the name cleared for trade mark use

↓

Decide if you will use a keyword-rich domain name and plan online marketing strategy

↓

Register domain names both in your brand name and in any keyword-rich domain

↓

File application to register name as a trade mark

↓

Get marketing input to decide on brand experience, tagline and communications

↓

At the same time commission visual branding such as logo and website, putting a legal agreement in place

↓

Register logo as a design

↓

Register logo and tagline as trade mark

Chapter 4: Key take-home messages

■ Choose a distinctive name for your business online so it's easier for people to remember you and find your site again.

■ Avoid using a generic or descriptive domain name – you could lose valuable business if customers mistake it for the name of one of your competitors.

■ Be consistent in your brand name and domain address to avoid confusion for users.

■ Knowing which keywords to target for your business in your website is vital to building an effective online brand.

Part Two
The Visual
Brand Identity

Chapter 5

How to own the copyright in your logo or other designs – and avoid the myths and misinformation

'Only one thing is impossible for God: to find any sense in any copyright law on the planet'
Mark Twain

As the brand name is how consumers identify a brand, it plays a central role in containing the brand's value. That's not to say that other elements, such as the brand's logo, packaging and designs are not important, too. They undoubtedly play a significant part in creating the brand's identity and may become the most ingrained image in consumers' consciousness.

Securing your rights in the name should precede identity creation and, once you are ready for branding, the book *Visual Hammer* by Laura Ries (Kindle, 2012) is a useful read for understanding the interaction between visual and verbal communication. She stresses the importance of having a visual hammer for your brand that is uniquely associated with it, in the same way that the Coca-Cola contour bottle brings to mind the Coca-Cola brand.

The laws governing visual identity

Copyright is the principal IP right to consider when it comes to your brand's visual identity. Other intellectual property rights also come into play, such as designs and trade marks, but they are of secondary importance in the visual elements of a brand.

Copyright is a wide-ranging subject and relevant to many creative and non-creative industries. Most visual brand elements – such as logos, packaging, and websites – are protected by copyright, even though it may also be possible to register some of these as designs or trade marks to secure added protection. (More information about copyright relating to websites and other online issues can be found in Chapters 6 and 7.)

Our example company, TTMC, plans to introduce a number of products, and wants to know to what extent its ideas will be protected against copying.

Definition of copyright

First, note that copyright protects 'works' (names and taglines are not protected by copyright but by trade marks). The copyright works that you may use for your brand include:

- books, brochures, letters and contracts
- music and sound recordings
- films and videos
- drawings, illustrations and photographs
- logos and packaging
- computer programs, databases and games.

An important point about copyright work is that it does not need to achieve a high standard in terms of quality in order to enjoy copyright. For example, if I scribbled a page of notes, I would own the copyright in the notes regardless of their quality. Another key point is that copyright protection arises automatically. This means that, unlike patents, trade marks and designs, it is not necessary to register the right in order to secure copyright ownership of it. However, don't let this lull you into a false sense of security.

One of the many myths surrounding copyright is that when you pay for a work, you become the copyright owner. This is not true. You would generally need to use an appropriate form of contract to secure the rights in a work because, although copyright arises automatically, it may well not arise in your favour. Generally, the default rules give copyright to the creator of a work.

Default rules for copyright ownership

The question of copyright ownership depends in part on who creates it, unless there is a specific written legal agreement to govern the matter.

One rule states that the creator of a work automatically becomes the 'first owner' of the copyright in the work, except where a work is created by an employee. Even if there is no written agreement with employees, specifying who is to own the copyright in any work they produce for an employer, under English law the employer is deemed to be the first owner of copyright if the work is created in the 'course of employment'.

An 'employee' means a member of staff on your payroll. Freelancers or self-employed contractors who work for you, whether on a permanent or occasional basis, are not your employees when it comes to the copyright default rule, and so you would not own copyright in any work they produce for you.

For this reason, our example company, TTMC, should ask a lawyer to assess the paperwork it uses with its freelance staff in order to ascertain whether copyright in work carried out by its freelancers belongs to TTMC and if it doesn't, TTMC should obtain appropriate assignments. For any new works to be created for the company, it makes sense to have a written agreement covering copyright-related matters such as ownership, moral rights (explained below) and use of pre-existing copyright works.

If you commission another business, be it a sole trader, partnership, company or educational establishment, to produce a copyright work for you, you will only own copyright in that work if the written agreement between you specifically states this. This agreement should be created before you commit to using someone's services for your project. Note that, in contract law, the time that you are regarded as legally bound to use someone's services may be much earlier than you realise. If you are no longer free to walk away, then unless the other party is willing to give you copyright, you have no right to demand it. Don't leave such discussions too late, or you will not be entitled to claim copyright, although the other party may indeed give it to you of their own accord.

In practice, if you are having an important product developed, such as an information technology project, it's important to deal with the rights in advance, no matter how agreeable your team seems to be to the idea of assigning the rights over to you. I've come across too many situations where the easy-going willingness of IT developers to assign rights turns into resistance when it comes to actually signing on the dotted line. The other party will often explain that it's their lawyers who have advised them against it.

Bear in mind that if you don't take steps to have ownership transferred to your own name in the early days, when the rights have little intrinsic value, once they do acquire value, other people are unlikely to readily agree to transfer the rights over to you without wanting some form of payment.

Rights of the copyright owner

Copyright, being a property right – like many other IP rights – can be sold, bought, given away or left to someone in a will. The copyright owner is the one entitled to 'exploit' the work, such as by copying elements of it and selling copies of the work to the public. The rights exclusively enjoyed by a copyright owner include renting or licensing the work to others, broadcasting it, transmitting it over the Internet, adapting it into other languages, and so on.

As Gavin, the owner of TTMC, intends to record an audio version of his book, he is free to do so if he's the copyright owner of the book and has not granted an exclusive licence to someone else to produce recordings. Otherwise, if he is restricted from exploiting his book in this way, or in other ways that he intends to commercialise it, he will need to seek the permission of the copyright owner or licensee.

This is something for Gavin to focus on when considering how to publish his book. Whether he goes down the road of self-publishing or finds a publisher, he should review the publising agreement to make sure he retains all the rights that his plans require him to retain. If he wants to be the one to produce translations of the book, then the publisher's exclusive right to produce translations must be negotiated out of the contract before Gavin accepts to be published by that particular publisher.

Similarly, as Gavin intends to produce CDs, podcasts, videos and eBooks to package aspects of his know-how and disseminate it to a wider audience, he should make sure the publishing contract does not preclude this. To earn revenues he would otherwise have not generated from a consulting business, Gavin should check that he can control all the necessary rights involved. He will also need a suitable agreement tailored for use when engaging assistance to create these materials.

If Gavin were to host a TTMC event and he was joined on stage by a third party who gave a talk as part of the event, that speaker would have public performance rights. If the event was recorded and Gavin later sold the video, he would be infringing the copyright of the other speaker if he had not secured the speaker's written consent. So it might be appropriate for Gavin to include, in the terms of a licence or assignment, provision for the speaker to receive a percentage of the profits made from video sales.

As always, it's easier to negotiate the relevant rights before you've engaged someone's services than afterwards. The best policy is to write your requirements into the agreement when you commission a work such as a website. If the agreement doesn't give you a full licence to use the work for all your intended purposes, you may later be charged a further fee for permissions to use it. For example, if you are having a professional photograph taken, agree with the photographer what uses you will be able to make of the photo in future – is it just for your website and social networking sites, or could you also use the photo if a journalist asked you for your image to accompany a magazine article about you?

Copying a substantial part of a work

Many people mistakenly assume that you can copy someone's work as long as you acknowledge and credit them as the author. If you take 'a substantial part' of a work, you will be infringing copyright in it. This is a trap for the unwary as, in some cases, even a very small part of a work may be deemed to be a substantial part of it. And it doesn't make it acceptable if you acknowledge the author.

Note that you may sometimes copy a large proportion of a work without infringing copyright, because it will not necessarily form a substantial part of the text in question. This would apply if the material was fairly generic. On the other hand, copying a small fraction of the whole work may sometimes be enough to infringe copyright in a work.

In one case, a judge had to decide whether a 20-second recording of a piece of music known as *Colonel Bogey* (where the whole song lasted four minutes) infringed copyright. In finding that it did, he said:

This reproduction is clearly a substantial part of Colonel Bogey ... *Anyone hearing it would know that it was the march called* Colonel Bogey, *and though it may be that it was not very prolonged in its reproduction, it is clearly, in my view, a substantial, a vital, and an essential part which is there reproduced.*

Unfortunately, there is no rule of thumb test for determining what uses you may make of a copyright work. So take care and, if necessary, seek legal advice before borrowing from a copyright work, especially if it's used for a commercial purpose, such as in a book you're writing.

If you don't have permission, and you don't have a defence under the 'fair dealing' exceptions, you would infringe the owner's copyright. The fair dealing defence is available if you are using an image for the purposes of review and criticism (such as to report an event in the news), or if it's purely for non-commercial research or private study. Similarly, there is no copyright infringement if copyright work is incidentally included in an artistic work, sound recording, film or broadcast (so-called 'passing shot' use). However, if music is deliberately included in a work (e.g. playing on a radio included in a scene in a film) its inclusion cannot be said to be incidental.

Making adaptations

The law clarifies some of the activities that it regards as copying, such as making an adaptation of it. So, if you've written a book and own the copyright and all rights in it, only you can authorise a translation of it into another language. And only you may create a play to dramatise the story in the novel. If anyone else were to go ahead and do this, they would be infringing your rights. This is a qualitative test not a quantitative one.

Case study: Hodgson and Jarvie

In the case of *Hodgson and Jarvie v. Isaac and Notting Hill Movies* (2011) a judge had to decide whether a film script of a book was an infringement of the book's copyright. This case is a good illustration of the concept of substantial copying. The decision turned on whether the film script (*Down Among the Dead Men*) of the book *Flipper's Side* was an adaptation of it. Only the copyright owner has the right to create an adaptation of a work. In deciding this question, Judge Birss said:

When the book and the DADM script are each considered as a whole, the DADM script is in fact very closely related to the book in terms of its plot, characters and the striking incidents and events which take place. The text is almost entirely different but nine episodes in the DADM script revolve around striking events present in Flipper's Side *and five more include notable events from* Flipper's Side *as important parts of the episode. In as much as it is possible or meaningful to quantify such things, in my judgement roughly half of the dramatic incidents in the DADM script derive from* Flipper's Side.

To conclude, the judge, having read both texts, decided the script amounted to a substantial copy of the book because the main characters, many of the settings and contexts in which the events took place and a good number of the incidents themselves were featured in the script.

While it is not possible to stop others copying your ideas, if you have a business providing educational materials, and someone else copies the ideas embodied within your teaching program in great detail, then the detailed copying could constitute infringement of your copyright in the materials even though they may have put the content into their own words.

What are moral rights?

As a general rule, the creator of a copyright work has the right to be identified as its creator. In the context of use of freelancers or agencies, this means they have the right to be identified as the creator of the work they produce for you. When you see a website or brochure attributing the design to a named designer, the designer is exercising his or her moral right to be identified as the creator of the work. This is regardless of whether or not the designer transfers copyright to you.

You don't need to give the designer permission to exercise their moral right and you could require the designer or other freelancer to waive it in your contract provided you do so before the contract is made. One downside with the designer's exercise of moral rights is that it could curb your freedom to adapt the designs later. You may also need to credit each time you use your own brand element. So if you acquire copyright, ask for a waiver of all moral rights. In industries which produce copyright content for clients (such as graphic design) or those which primarily rely on copyright (such as the music, video games or technology industries), waiving moral rights by legal agreement with freelancers is of fundamental importance as it's unlikely the agency would want the freelancer to attribute the work to themselves.

Agencies using freelance designers

As the default rules provide that self-employed staff such as freelancers own copyright in work they produce for their 'employers' it is doubly important that businesses who produce copyright works for others and who sub-contract or use freelancers have an appropriate agreement covering copyright ownership, moral rights, and so on, with those supplying services to them.

It is possible to secure a transfer of copyright after the work has been created, but only if the freelancer is happy to assign it to you. If the agency is not in a position to pass on the necessary rights to its clients, its reputation could suffer dramatically.

Case study: R. Griggs & Co

In the case of *R. Griggs & Co and Airwair Ltd v. Ross Evans and Raben Footwear Pty* in 2003, an ad agency had used a freelancer (Evans), to produce a new logo for its client (Griggs). Evans's brief was to combine Griggs's existing Dr Martens and Airwair logos into one new logo. He duly did the work and supplied the new logo to Griggs via the ad agency. The question arose as to who owned copyright in the new logo when Evans tried to sell it to Griggs's competitors.

The court decided that the freelancer owned the copyright in the new logo due to the default rules mentioned above. He had created the logo, he was not an employee of the agency and had not agreed in writing to assign his copyright to the ad agency. However, the court felt that there were very special reasons why Evans should be prevented from selling the logo to Griggs's competitors.

Specifically, the court said: 'Logos are so fundamental to a company's identity and branding that it would be inappropriate to allow Evans to sell the logo to a third party, even though he was the owner of the copyright'.

If the issue had involved something other than a logo, say a special drawing for their brochure rather than a logo, the result is unlikely to have gone in Griggs's favour.

The parties incurred considerable legal fees to fight this out in court. In practice, only the wealthy can afford to argue when things go wrong. A small business owner or agency faced with the same situation would be unlikely to afford to protest in such a way. And remember, court decisions depend on the facts and circumstances of the particular case, as well as on a host of other matters which it is difficult to control, such as the skill of the lawyers involved, the attitude of the judge and the other side's financial resources.

The moral of this case is to ask questions, and to make sure your agency shows you a signed agreement from any freelancers working for the agency on your project.

Why you need copyright in your logo

In the case of logos, it's important to have copyright assigned to you because if anyone were to copy the logo, it's only the copyright owner who could legitimately complain. As it's likely to be you who would want to object rather than the designer who created the logo, you need to own the copyright.

The legal system will require proof of your ownership if you want to sue. You would have to prove that the designer of the logo actually assigned it to you in writing. If you can't show that you are the copyright owner, you will be hampered in your efforts to stop a third party infringing on the copyright in your logo.

Clearly, then, a verbal agreement from your designer that you could use the copyright would not be legally effective. And if you weren't able to track down the designer, you would have a problem in enforcing your rights. Again, this highlights the importance of having written agreements in place before you commission your designer. (You may still be able to have the copyright assigned to you after the work is completed if you ask for it, but it's pretty likely that you'll have to pay for the privilege.)

Physical objects and ownership of copyright are often separate

A fundamental point about copyright is that ownership of the physical object (book, software, CD or painting) and ownership of copyright in it are frequently in separate hands. Therefore, it is not the owner of the physical object who has the right to license its use. You need permission from the owner of the copyright.

There are many peculiarities of copyright law to be aware of. For example, if you took a photograph and in it was prominently featured somebody else's copyright work, such as their logo or paintings, you would be infringing the copyright of the owner of the logo or paintings.

Where the copyright work involves a piece of music, there will be at least two owners of copyright. There is the owner of the sound recording and also the owner of the copyright in the underlying music composition. (Indeed, the music composition in turn is likely to comprise the instrumental element of the music itself as well as the lyrics). Bear in mind, then, that if you wanted permission to use the music within your branding, you would need permission from all the copyright owners. A song is owned by the music publisher, while the recording of the song is owned by the label, as are the artists' rights (performance rights).

Sometimes the creator of copyright may be unwilling to transfer copyright to you; other times they may be willing to transfer the copyright only if you pay a premium. If ownership of copyright is important to you, discuss it when you are still free to walk away and find someone else to do the work for you. By considering ownership issues each time a piece of work is to be created for your business, and having appropriate agreements available to use for addressing ownership or licensing issues, you will be well placed to protect your business on a day-to-day basis as new projects are implemented.

Distinctive branding

Focusing on copyright ownership and exclusive rights is the way to achieve uniqueness in your branding. For example, if you use music in your branding and you own the copyright (perhaps the music was created especially for you), it means nobody else can use it. The music will evoke your brand only. Similarly, if you use photographs in which you own the copyright, nobody else will be able to use those images.

The benefit of basing dominant imagery for your brand on copyright elements that belong to you rather than to stock libraries or third parties, is that you can genuinely stand out from the crowd and avoid looking generic.

Endeavouring to use your own copyright music rather than using royalty-free music helps you avoid being one of many users. Similarly, if you use film footage and ensure you own the rights to it, you don't risk finding that another brand is licensing the same footage that you wanted to be associated with your brand.

When considering copyright, think about whether you will be able to use all the materials that belong to third parties and that you are currently using as part of your brand image – songs, photographs, footage? Can you use them in all media, all formats, and worldwide? If you license an iconic song, will you be able to afford world Internet rights for viral ads? You don't want to be forced into abandoning an iconic element of your brand campaign midstream at a time when you are growing the brand.

Using other people's content (such as stock images) may be cheaper, but you might be just one of many people using it. This might be acceptable in the early days of your business, but in due course you will want to give a more substantial impression of your brand than you can evoke with generic imagery. To avoid your branding looking 'downmarket', consider taking your own photographs or choosing images from stock libraries which have a low number of downloads.

> Let's say that Gavin decides that TTMC will use its own copyright and design elements as far as possible to create a distinctive and unique brand. TTMC has a very good design agency that is willing to provide services on the basis that Gavin's business will own the rights. So TTMC will engage the agency once a new name is found for the business, and in the meantime asks to see its terms of business.
>
> Although Gavin is good friends with his designer and thinks it unlikely the designer would enforce his copyright ownership against his business, he understands the importance of being businesslike and using a legal contract. It's not a question of whether he trusts or likes his designer. In business, anything can happen. People move away, you lose touch with them, new management teams can come in, and so on, all of which can sweep away even genuine gentlemen's agreements.

Although there is no registration system in place in the UK to secure copyright, it's a good idea to have evidence satisfactory to a court of law of the date of creation of the copyright. You may have been told that it's enough to put your material in an envelope and post it to yourself to prove the date of creation of a copyright work, but this is a myth. Also for international protection, there are advantages in registering your copyright with the US Patent and Trademark Office (USPTO) although it is not compulsory to do so.

Who should own copyright?

In terms of when it's appropriate to ask for copyright and when it's not, for brand elements such as your logo, the copyright should be transferred to you without question. There is no particular reason why a designer would want to retain the copyright in it. Similarly, where written materials are created for your business, the copywriter is usually willing to transfer copyright to you. These are not controversial situations where the creator is justified in wanting to retain copyright ownership.

On the other hand, if someone is writing software for your business, they may have some justification for not being so willing to transfer ownership of it to you, or to only do so by charging a higher amount. For instance, they might need to use the generic underlying software platform to create works for other clients.

So, the question comes down to the reasons why copyright should be granted or retained, or moral rights asserted or waived.

However, there is still a lot you can do to protect your position even where the other party is not willing to transfer copyright to you. By securing a written licence (permission) to use the work for all the purposes for which you may want to use it within your business, you could potentially get all the rights you need. We'll look at different aspects of licensing in more detail in the next two chapters.

Permission to use copyright works

When obtaining copyright permissions you need to know what questions to ask, how to track down the copyright owner, and so on. This can be a complex process and you may need specialist help.

It may not always be obvious who has the right to give you permission to use a copyright work. For example, if you wanted permission to use a photograph or music that you initially saw on someone's website, it's very unlikely that the website owner would be the one who could give you permission to use it, although they may be able to give you information about whom to approach in order to use that particular copyright work.

Copyright ownership can change hands many times. So, remember this when trying to trace the copyright owner for any permissions. In practice, it is often difficult, even for professionals, to know who owns the copyright in a given work at any particular time, and it may take time to research this. The copyright rules only tell you who owned the copyright at the point the work was created and what formalities are required to assign (i.e. transfer) copyright. From there on, you need to trace what happened to it.

Joint copyright

Another point to beware of is unwittingly creating a joint copyright work when others collaborate on your project. Again, address the copyright situation by agreeing the details in writing before embarking on a project. Otherwise, you risk an attempt by others to claim joint copyright over your copyright work.

Case study: Locksley Brown

In the case *Locksley Brown v Mcasso Music Production Ltd,* joint copyright arose in favour of a session performer (Brown) who had played a significant role in adapting the lyrics of a song composed by the company for a television commercial. This meant that the session performer's copyright had been infringed when Mcasso used the song on its website.

As the performer was a freelancer and not the employee of Mcasso Music Production Ltd, he owned copyright in his contribution and therefore joint copyright arose. Mcasso Music Production could easily have avoided this result by using an appropriate written agreement securing an assignment of rights to the production company.

The problem with owning copyright jointly is that unless you can separate your contribution from that of the other party, such as you'd be able to do if one of you wrote two chapters of a book, while the other wrote ten, it would be impossible for either of you to exploit the work without the other party's agreement. If you could separate your contributions, you could each walk away with your own part of the work and be free to exploit your work.

Intellectual property rights in practice

Design protection

Think about the importance of the way things look and why you bought a particular pair of shoes, watch or necklace, and you'll understand why you would want to protect your brand's visual differentiators.

Registering the shape of unique designs such as the iPod, a perfume bottle, fashion garments like handbags, or pieces of furniture such as chairs or coffee tables, or packaging such as plastic bottles for washing liquid are all important ways in which to own the visual aspects of your brand.

Specific elements – such as the labels you apply to packaging, or a special font that's unique to your visual identity, the colour of letters, your logo, visual features of your website or the surface decoration on products like textiles or wallpaper – could all be distinctive aspects of your designs to protect through design registration. By registering the more important ones as designs, you secure stronger rights in them.

A good way to understand the difference between design protection and patents is this: the visual features of something like the Dyson vacuum cleaner will be protected by design registration, while the way it functions without a bag is something that is protected by patents.

Design registration: UK or EU design registration

It is possible to register designs such as logos solely in the UK or in all 27 countries in the EU by using what's called a 'Community design'. Either way, the registration lasts for five years and is renewable for a maximum of 25 years. However, unless a design is registered within a year of being made public, it is too late to ever register it as a design.

The overriding point when deciding whether to register a design is the importance and longevity of the design. For example, many fashion garments tend not to be registered because the designs are unlikely to endure beyond a couple of seasons. Such designs may have adequate protection under unregistered design law (see below).

Design registration does make it easier to stop others making, using or selling your design as depicted in the drawings of your design. If you don't register the design, either because you were too late and failed to register within the first year of the design being made public, or because you did not consider that it merited registration, you still have unregistered design right protection.

At TTMC, Gavin's desk accessory product has a distinctive shape. He can protect the rights to the shape by registering it as a design. However, for such a registration to be effective, it would not be sufficient to file photographs of the finished product. Gavin therefore needs to use a more tactical approach, such as using fine line drawings to give good representations of the design features. Registering each separate element of the design as well as the overall design is the approach that will give the greatest chance of success when it comes to preventing copycat designs.

The benefit of registering a design is that it deters others from copying your designs if they search the design registers and find out that you have protected the design. It is far easier to enforce your rights if the design is registered than if you need to rely on unregistered rights. There is no need to prove copying.

When someone wants to object to copying of registered designs, the validity of the design registration is likely to be questioned. That's when you have to show that the design feature you registered is new or 'novel' and has 'individual character', in other words, that your design is original and not commonplace. This is a different test from the one that applies to copyright where 'originality' simply means that it must not have been copied.

A design registration potentially offers Gavin an effective tool to combat infringing copycat designs, provided the application itself is done properly with copying in mind. The goal should be to represent the designs in such a way as to ring-fence the most important elements of the designs from copycats.

Although using a series of photographs or even just one photograph of the desk accessory design may be good enough for registration purposes, it is unlikely to be effective if someone challenges the registration. If it would be relatively easy to 'design around' an existing registration, then it would be a waste of money to have registered it. Rather the registration should aim to encapsulate those features of the design that Gavin wants to prevent others from copying.

Using IP rights strategically can be the way in which to own valuable assets. Shapes are difficult to register as trade marks.

Shape registration and trade marks

Gavin's desk accessory for time management is something he is interested in obtaining maximum protection over. So although the accessory has an unusual shape, it's not worth trying to trade mark it because the test laid down by the law to secure trade mark protection of a shape makes it necessary to show that the shape is associated in consumers' minds as a 'designation of origin'.

Coca-Cola was able to show that its bottle shape was a designation of origin because it used design registration for its distinctive bottle shape to stop anyone else using it for some 14 years. During this period, Coca-Cola used its large advertising budget to associate the bottle shape in the public's mind as its 'sign'. By the time the design registration had expired, Coca-Cola's trade mark for the bottle shape was in force. It was possible to register it because Coca-Cola was able to show that when people saw the bottle shape on its own they equated it with goods originating from Coca-Cola. In other words, the bottle shape had become an identifier.

Now that Coca-Cola has a trade mark, it has a permanent, exclusive right over its distinctive bottle shape. Provided it renews its trade mark and continues to use the bottle shape, nobody else may ever use the same bottle shape. This is powerful IP indeed. Coca-Cola is a very good example of a company that has used IP laws to good effect to create a very strong brand.

If Gavin wants to emulate Coca-Cola, he will need to focus on design registration, and try to gradually build up recognition in the shape of the desk accessory in the 25 years of design registration that the business will have. During that time it must vigorously promote the shape as an identifier. Possibly, the availability of social media platforms makes it possible for a small business without a huge advertising budget to achieve such a task.

Trade mark protection of visual identity

Trade marks are relevant to protecting visual identity, should you want to register your logo or other designs as a trade mark. From this it should be noted that each type of IP right (copyright, design, and trade mark) provides slightly different protection over the same elements of a brand. The way to have strong IP protection in your business is to secure as many of these IP rights as possible. Each right will protect you in different ways and situations.

Under the 'default' provisions in the legislation, ownership of copyright will be with the creator of the work, but the design rights belong to the party who commissions the designs. So, if you commissioned a designer to produce a logo or other designs for you – as in Nike's 'swoosh' – you would own the rights in the designs. On the other hand, the designer would own the rights in copyright unless you agreed in writing that the copyright was to belong to you.

Consider whether to register any designs early on, as the right to do so is time limited. You should also secure ownership of the copyright in the designs so that you are able to sue third parties for using the logo if necessary.

In the Digital Opportunity report (May 2011), led by Professor Ian Hargreaves, a raft of ways to reduce the complexity of copyright law and facilitate the use of copyright works was recommended. Reforms being proposed to the copyright legislation are aiming to make it easier for businesses to negotiate their way around copyright in certain contexts. A review of design laws is also pending.

Conclusion

TTMC, our example business, has been using a number of freelancers without using specific written agreements. Some of these freelancers were hired through platforms like Elance, where the platform protects your interests and gives the copyright ownership to you. However, for other freelancers Gavin will need to obtain assignments of rights. Copyright ownership is very important to him, given his desire to create products. It's also important for his contract with his publishing company to be examined, as many copyright contracts assign the rights to the publisher and it's the publisher who has the right to create adaptations of the content. Gavin will also need to review the contract with his proposed design agency in order to ensure he will own all the copyright that is generated, and so that his design agency only uses elements in his branding that Gavin will be able to own or use exclusively so as to retain a distinctive look to his brand.

Chapter 5: Key take-home messages

■ The creator of a 'work' automatically owns the copyright.

■ Be aware that the copyright in a work remains with the creator even if you have paid for the creation of the work.

■ Have in place a written agreement assigning you the copyright of any work you commission before you commit to using an outside agency's services.

■ Make sure you have full licence to use the work for all your intended purposes.

Chapter 6

What you always wanted to know about commissioning a website but didn't know who to ask

'It used to be expensive to make things public and cheap to make them private. Now it's expensive to make things private and cheap to make them public' Clay Shirky, Internet scholar and professor at NYU

In the days when businesses were just getting savvy to the Internet's potential, you might have struggled to find a competitor online, but today you're often lucky if there are fewer than a million web pages in your area of business all competing for position.

So, although the Internet presents huge opportunities, you need to distinguish your business from a crowd of innovators, imitators and hobbyists. The competitive environment and its fast-changing nature can easily soak up funds.

Our example company, TTMC, operates online only and it intends to continue in that form in the medium term. Eventually, it may source a small office for core staff to work from, but its website will always be its main shop window.

As an online business, it wants to take advantage of the fact that people's first port of call, when it comes to finding information about products and services, is the Internet. TTMC sells to a global audience and its target market is online. Having a local presence will be less relevant, as Gavin's business model will shift from delivering a consultancy service to licensing others worldwide to offer the services. He will also be delivering some of his knowledge in productised form. The business will also use some of its products to create new offerings supported by a reduced service element. This means that, in some cases, the service element will be delivered via Skype and other electronic mediums. Where a physical presence is required, Gavin's licensed practitioners will deliver services in individual countries.

The Internet therefore presents the possibility of multiplying Gavin's customer base overnight, and Gavin will be positioning his business to meet the needs of a much wider audience than those within his immediate locality (London).

Marketing

First, it's important for Gavin to be clear about how he will promote the brand online. This decision has a number of ramifications on the type of site he might commission.

Let's look at how you might use the Internet to promote your business, generate more hits and increase potential sales.

There are a number of different viewpoints. If you engage an SEO consultant, they will advocate throwing your efforts into optimising your site for search engines, ensuring a high ranking – in other words, your site's name will appear right at the top of a list of sites given in answer to a web query that features your keywords. Some Internet marketers may advise purchasing keywords through Google AdWords or using social media. Others will recommend you focus on uncovering your 'niche' and targeting a small but loyal audience. A more traditional PR firm might advise you to look at having some kind of value-added giveaway to stimulate traffic to your website.

Who's right? They all are. As in traditional marketing, there is no 'one true way'. Most web businesses will need a mixed approach to increase online sales and leads, and to get more business.

While it's important for all businesses to have a niche, the Internet presents unique opportunities to narrow your focus and have a 'micro' niche. You have a wider pool of potential customers to target. A business that would be unsustainable if located in one country could be viable – and potentially extremely profitable – as an Internet business. So it's worth considering whether there is a tiny gap in the market that Gavin could fill when doing keyword research. Targeting that gap online may be a smarter way of getting customers on board than trying to promote all the various ways in which the business can meet the needs of people seeking time management services. Once the customers are found, Gavin has the opportunity to sell additional services to them.

Also, if you want people online to be talking about your business, you need to get involved in the conversation. Not every social networking tool may be appropriate for your business. But you do need an understanding of what's out there and how it could potentially raise awareness of your services and help grow your company. Working out how to engage with customers on their own turf, and lead them to your website will be an important consideration.

Internet forums

A good Internet forum is a public 'meeting space' where like-minded people can come together to discuss their interests in a friendly and supportive environment. Some forums may have thousands of users, all interested in the very products your company happens to market. Rather than going to the expense of developing a forum from scratch, why not start by using the facilities that Facebook and LinkedIn provide, and then see if you want to build your own.

When participating in other people's forums, think carefully about the way in which you choose to engage with potential customers. For example, don't use a pseudonym and start promoting your website – it's the digital equivalent of heading down to the pub and handing out business cards randomly to strangers.

Bear in mind, too, that there is legislation in place – the Consumer Protection from Unfair Trading Regulations 2008 – which is aimed at preventing 'buzz marketing' or 'astroturfing', as the practice is known in the US. Take care not to pretend to be a consumer and not to give your own business laudatory feedback. Falling on the wrong side of the law carries a fine and even if no prosecution is brought against you, a practice deemed illegal by the Advertising Standards Authority (ASA) could lead to other undesirable consequences for your business. For example, insurers may disclaim liability, suppliers may argue they have a right to walk away from particular contracts, other bodies such as the Consumers' Association could become involved.

Quite apart from the potentially reputation-damaging issues, this kind of marketing is almost always a failure and serves only to alienate potential customers. If you want to engage with forum users, transparency is the key.

Make a profile in your own name or your company's name, include links to your official website and make an effort to contribute useful information to the forum. By establishing yourself as a trustworthy authority on a specific topic, you can grow the profile of your business.

Blogs

A corporate blog can be a great way to engage with your customers and give them an insight into the day-to-day operations of your business. It's also flexible and it allows you to comment on events or announcements, or even potential bad news about your company in a friendly, easily accessible and less formal way than a traditional press release. A blog is an important addition to the website and in Gavin's case will help him build ranking for his chosen domain name. He should enable comments on his blog entries, to allow him to have a dialogue with readers.

Microsites

A microsite is a website that is separate from your main business website and has its own domain. For example, if VandelayClothing.com is your primary website, which advertises a range of clothing available for order, and you want to give prominence to a Christmas sale without distracting from your core site and changing its content, a microsite might be the way to do it.

In this kind of situation, you might look at creating the microsite VandelayChristmas.com, which focuses on the specific festive sale. An added benefit of this is the relevance of 'contextual advertising', which involves advertising on other websites depending on the keyword. By going down this route you could, for example, grab the attention of Internet users who are searching for Christmas information with targeted advertising about your specific Christmas website.

Social networks

We'll look at social media in depth in Chapter 9, but here, suffice to say that in general terms, a social networking site is an Internet website that allows you to connect and interact with people with similar interests. One of the most prominent social networking sites is Facebook, which currently has over 900 million members: if it were a country, it would be the third biggest in the world.

Your business cannot afford to ignore Facebook and microblogging sites like Twitter. However, it's important to think carefully about where you position links to these sites on your own website, as you don't want to encourage traffic to move away from your site when it has just landed there.

Get friendly with the search engines

The goal online is to have a site that appears more prominently than its competitors' sites, so that when potential customers are searching for the products or services you offer, you are more likely to appear among the search engine's results.

The good thing about search engines is that they do a lot of the work for you. Unlike the traditional hard-copy Yellow Pages, you don't need to get listed for particular search results – Google will seek out your site and add it to its database, provided the site is set up properly. But there also are several things you can do to make it easier for search engines to find you, and potentially to index you higher in their rankings.

Although complicated Flash graphics can make a website look great, search engines actually prefer text. The automated search engine 'spiders' – programs that follow, or 'crawl' links throughout the Internet, grabbing content from sites and adding it to search engine indexes – can also find it difficult to understand pictures, so if your DVD-selling movie review website opens with a series of images of popcorn, projectors and film footage, it may look stunning but it won't mean much to the search engine.

To appear in the search results, you'd do better to feature a clear text description of your movie review website, describing the reviews you offer and the DVDs you have for sale. The search engine will then be able to 'crawl' your site and determine that your website offers movie reviews and sells associated DVDs.

Try to think of the search engines the same way you'd think of a person looking at your website. Make the content clear and easy to understand and have a simple, easy-to-follow structure.

Content is king

Users – be they existing customers or potential customers – appreciate a high-quality website. More than that, however, they look for content. The slickest website in the world won't win many fans if the content isn't of equal quality.

Keywords and clever use of Google will bring customers into your 'digital storefront', but good content encourages them to stick around a while and check out the merchandise.

Your content needs to stand out – be remarkable, even – in order to attract links, visitors and to enable you to be heard above the din.

Bearing in mind the pivotal role that the website will have in Gavin's business, it's just as important for him to get the details right and lay out his e-store properly online as it would be if he were taking on physical premises and kitting out a shop. Despite the fact that everything on the Internet is intangible, Gavin should still take great care to have proper contracts in place with his team.

A successful web project should take account of the marketing considerations outlined earlier while avoiding the temptation to sign up to expensive ongoing contracts for SEO, social media marketing, and the like.

Adopting a 'buyer beware' approach rather than an informal one is very important in order to achieve a successful website development outcome.

There are three key aspects to securing the rights you need in the website:

1. the 'look and feel' of the website;

2. the underlying software technology;

3. the content featured on the site, such as images, videos, words, etc.

Getting your website under way

The first objective is to find a team of specialists to help you realise your vision. A good web designer will design the site, and a talented graphic designer can help you stand out from the crowd with an eye-catching logo and artwork. For websites that collect information and have an online shop or give visitors access to useful tools, a web developer will need to be involved in writing the software behind it.

Web designer or web developer?

A client who commissioned a web designer to build a website with an e-commerce store was not too clued-up on the distinction between web designers and web developers. Consequently, she didn't quiz the web designer on whether he would be outsourcing any of the work and, if so, what. The site's launch was to coincide with the television appearance of the business's founders, and it was hoped that this exposure would help increase sales of its products. In the end, the web designer was unable to find a web developer to build the e-store as all his contacts were busy.

When you have a time-sensitive requirement, engage the skills of the person who is most able to help you achieve your desired outcome. In this case, a web developer should have been put in charge of the project, not a web designer.

In the grand scheme of things, the visual appeal of a site is not the main consideration. You wouldn't show a builder a few pictures of houses you liked and then leave him to get on with it. You'd want to see detailed plans, to ensure it met your practical requirements.

Likewise, you need to focus on the details of the site you want built. How many links do you want from the menu bar, what is to feature on the home page, what pathways do you want to provide for the different audiences who will land on your site? Otherwise, you risk getting a stunningly beautiful site – but one that doesn't actually work in the way you want it to. For instance, it might be built using technology that makes it difficult for search engines to crawl the site. If you want to attract business from your website, make sure you explain this very clearly to your web designer, so you don't end up with a site built with Flash technology that is not search-engine friendly.

Pitfalls of website design

A friend of a friend of mine had a beautiful, very clever-looking website that was his pride and joy. However, he was puzzled as to why he did not appear on the first page of Google in the search results. For several years, he ploughed on, without getting as much business from the Internet as he had hoped, despite doing everything he personally could to try to help his site get ranking on the search engines. He eventually found out the problem was down to the way his website was constructed. So, he paid for a new website, at a cost he could ill afford, and soon saw more business coming his way from online enquiries.

Gavin's site will require an e-commerce platform and a blog, so it makes sense for him to put a developer in overall charge. As the person commissioning a piece of copyright work is disadvantaged by contracting the work orally, and the fact that many Internet professionals do not use written agreements, Gavin would be advised to look for a professional company that has terms of business so he understands the basis on which it quotes. As the seller of a service is responsible for having written terms, Gavin needn't go to the expense of producing a contract for his developer. Instead, he should put the onus on the developer to produce contract terms for review before he formally engages its services.

The purpose of a specification

For the site Gavin has in mind, it's a good idea for him to get the details of the requirements incorporated into a specification rather than commissioning the site on the basis of a proposal. A proposal is essentially a sales brochure; a specification, on the other hand, describes the site in detail. Having a specification means that, if there were a dispute, it would then be easier to analyse the paperwork and understand what type of site was meant to be delivered.

In practice, if a website project fails to deliver the expected benefits, people tend not to escalate their website problems into a legal dispute because of the expense involved. There are many ways in which website projects can deliver less than positive results, but once you've had the site built, if you're not happy with it, it's too late. You're into potential litigation or dispute by then.

Getting proper help and advice with a website project before appointing a developer costs a fraction of the amount you'd need to pay a lawyer to resolve a dispute. It's also more likely to help you achieve a successful outcome, so don't scrimp on taking advice.

Similarly, don't dismiss the idea of commissioning a specification simply because of the expense involved. Yes, you'll need to pay for this as a specification is rather like a set of architect's drawings. But another advantage of having a specification is that you can use it to get like-for-like quotations from web designers.

When rebranding, people often lose the search engine benefits that they enjoyed with their old name, so it's important for TTMC to quiz its proposed developers to make sure they know how to do things like redirecting pages of their old website, which had built up ranking, to the new site. These requirements could then be incorporated into the specification.

If you want to reduce the costs, one approach might be to talk to developers, and then once you've identified one you may want to work with, pay them to draw up a specification as a prelude to awarding the project. You'll then be clear on the type of site you will be receiving and you can use the specification to get like-for-like quotes from other developers.

Your platform: open source or proprietary?

In terms of platforms, be aware of the implications of using open-source or proprietary software such as a closed-source content management system. Proprietary software locks you in to using your developer's content management system. Open source software, though free, can be expensive to maintain and update if it is not well supported by a ready supply of developers. WordPress is an example of an open-source software that is well supported, and therefore in widespread use for websites. But even if someone will be developing a WordPress site for you, so you have a platform which makes it easy for you to find developers able to maintain it, it's still important to consider the quality of the hosting you will get, security issues, and the competence of the person who is to do the work.

Identifying your website requirements

In the case study highlighted earlier, about the problems of the client's website not meeting her needs in time to coincide with the television appearance of its founder, the web designer had built a static HTML site. This meant that in order to add pages or change the words on a page it was necessary to know how to use a special programming language (HTML).

This type of site may be acceptable if you want a beautiful 'brochure' site that acts as a shop window, one that you will not need to change very often, but it was a completely inappropriate choice for the client as she wanted to advertise online using AdWords (more about this in Chapter 10).

To do this, she needed to be able to add fresh pages and alter existing pages in order to test what worked and what didn't. She also wanted her site to rank highly in the search engines, so the facility to add more pages was indispensable. There was nothing wrong in what the designer had done. The problem arose because the client had not taken the time to understand the issues and spell out her requirements. The reason for this was partly due to her lack of knowledge about what she required. She was expecting the web designer to read her mind and decide what she needed.

Questions about how you will be able to extend the site are also relevant, as are the running costs and likely charges for further work required. If you want to allow visitors to your site to download content, and you want to be able to take contact information, these and a host of other details should be discussed in advance. Recording details in writing before commissioning the site is the best way of achieving a successful outcome.

Related points to raise before awarding the work to a developer include whether someone else will be able to maintain the site. If it's your developer's proprietary software that will be used, how easy will it be to move the site so someone else can take care of your needs?

What would be involved in moving the site if you wanted to do so in the future? Make sure you understand this before you award the work. The developer has every incentive to respond and agree to your requests when he or she wants to win the work. Even with a WordPress site, moving the site from one host to another entails some work, the extent of which will depend on the size of your website. Even for a small website, it might involve at least half a day of a developer's time to do the move and testing.

Maintenance charges

A cause of dissatisfaction with your website could be that the maintenance charges are too high. You may want to move away from your website developer once the site is built because they lack the skills or speed of response you require. That's when you realise it's not straightforward to move a site. So think about the platform before you commission the site, to assess the extent to which you will be tied to your web developer. You don't want to be stuck in an unsatisfactory situation simply because you can't afford to pay a large amount to another developer to either move the site or build you a new one. Have an exit plan in case you want to move away from your developer.

Copyright and ownership of 'look and feel'

Websites comprise many different types of copyright work and can involve complex technologies. An important aspect of your due diligence should be to ensure you don't infringe on third parties' rights by using content without all the relevant permissions.

Even if the copyright in the underlying software that makes your website function is not going to be transferred to you, make sure you get a proper licence to use it, as well as copyright in your website's 'look and feel' – in other words, its visual aspects.

If the developer is reluctant to give you those rights, then he or she should give you a comprehensive licence to use those elements of your website's look and feel for all commercial purposes, including the right to transfer rights to a third party (which would be helpful should you sell the business). Protecting your business involves negotiating details such as this at the outset, and making sure that any drawings and photographs used on your website, or as part of your brand identity, are properly licensed. (Licensing of images and Creative Commons is discussed in the next chapter.)

It's far easier to protect yourself, by making sure your web designer has not incorporated any infringing content into your site, than it is to try to chase them to pay you damages if they did use material that infringes on third parties' rights.

Case study: Antiquesportfolio.com

In the case *Antiquesportfolio.com v. Rodney Fitch*, a web designer had produced a website for a client that incorporated infringing content.

The design agency had used small icons of images drawn from *Miller's Antiques Encyclopedia* in designing a website for Antiquesportfolio.com. However, Antiquesportfolio.com decided not to take delivery of the website because, in its view, the taking of images from the Encyclopedia without a licence infringed the rights in the photos.

Rodney Fitch, the web design agency, argued that the images were too small to infringe copyright. However, the court decided in favour of Antiquesportfolio.com and agreed that it did not need to pay for the website or take delivery of it in view of the fact that if it did so, it would be infringing the rights of third parties by using the website.

Owning the copyright in your website, artwork or content – including your print and advertising copy – gives you more freedom to manoeuvre, without the risk of infringing copyright.

If there are elements of your website that you do not legally own, you will need a written licence to use the copyright works. The licence should cover all the uses you want to make of these elements in future. Otherwise, you would need to pay every time you used the work in a way that was not permitted under your licence in order to avoid infringing on the rights of the copyright owner. Also, you would not be allowed to combine elements of these works with other content without the copyright owner's permission.

The permission or licence should address how much you will have to pay, how long you may use the work, whether you can use it elsewhere in your marketing materials, and so on. Working out the licence provisions can be a complex job, but it's much simpler to cover the details in your initial licence than it is to track down the owner in a few years' time if you need to extend the rights. This is particularly important if you're having software developed for your business. Do you want to license third parties to use it? If so, discuss this with your proposed developer before you award them the work.

As copyright laws are unduly complicated, licensing terms – such as under Creative Commons (see below) – are, in turn, complicated. Many people don't know whether an image found on a Google image search or elsewhere on the web is protected by copyright and, if so, whether permission to use it would be forthcoming. It's necessary to have quite a good grasp of copyright law, licensing, as well as Creative Commons licences to know what use you may make of images.

Licensing of images and other works

A licence is a contractual agreement between the copyright owner and the user, giving permission for the use of the copyrighted work. So, if you search on an image library like iStock, read the licence terms before you buy the image, to make sure it covers your intended use.

A good starting point regarding copyright and the use of images, is to allay the common misconception that simply because an image is widely used, it can be used by others legally. This is incorrect. No matter how commonplace the photo, or image featured in a photo, the copyright in it still belongs to the copyright owner unless it's in the public domain. Tracking down the copyright owner for every image you are currently using is time-consuming and expensive. From a practical point of view, it may be simpler to buy images from stock libraries.

Commercial image libraries

The most well-known commercial image libraries are iStock, Getty Images or Shutterstock, and these give an indication of different licences available. The licences vary according to how you intend to use the photographs. For instance, in the case of Getty Images, if you intended to use a photo many times for multiple projects you would need a royalty-free licence. There is even a specific licence for using the product in an editorial collection.

These commercial libraries charge per licence, and the extent of the charges will depend on the scope of your intended use. As an alternative to buying stock library images, you can source images licensed under 'Creative Commons'.

Creative Commons

Creative Commons, or 'Copyleft' as it is sometimes referred to, is a form of licensing in which the creator of the piece surrenders some, but not all, of their rights under copyright law. There are several different types of Creative Commons Licence.

The most permissive form allows the person copying the work the same freedoms as the author, including the right to use the work, share the work, modify the work and then distribute the modified work. The big catch to this is that if you use a work under this type of licence, you cannot receive any financial gain or profit from it and you cannot restrict others from using it. If you tried to do so, you would be violating the original licence.

On the Internet, if you wanted to use content from other sites that use this type of licence, you would have to license any further work under these same conditions. Choosing content that has this type of licence is good for blogging but would not be well suited to a website where you are running a business.

Paying a fee for a licence gives you permission to use that image, but the copyright of that image does not belong to you and you must comply with the conditions of the licence that the creator sets out.

One condition that might be applied to a licence is 'Attribution', which means that others can copy, display and distribute the copyrighted work, but only if they give a credit in the way the creator requests. Another condition that might apply to a licence is 'Share Alike', which means the creator allows others to distribute derivative works (i.e. works based on the original) only under a licence identical to that governing the original work.

A 'Non-Commercial' condition may apply to a licence, meaning that others can copy, display and distribute the work, but only for non-commercial purposes. Lastly, a 'No Derivative Works' condition may apply, which means that others can copy, display and distribute the work but may not create derivative works based on it. These different conditions can be mixed and matched to suit the licensor's needs.

Google Images

Google's advanced image search gives you information about the copyright position of Google Images.

A Google Image search lets you search exclusively for photos with Creative Commons licences. When clicking through to the image you will usually find information about the type of Creative Commons licence granted. You may also select the type of licence you would like to search for, and so your results will be restricted to images marked with CC or your chosen type of licence. You can then use the image if you comply with the terms.

Flickr and other sites

Flickr is an image library with a large Creative Commons image database. If you have a look at their licensing page, you will see that they list the different Creative Commons licences they provide and the respective databases for each type of licence.

Database rights

As you are likely to be taking contact details on your website and developing a mailing list, a list of customers, or any other collection of materials that you have either created or that you want to draw from, you should bear in mind database right.

Such databases may enjoy copyright protection but even if they don't, the material will very likely be protected by database right.

The definition of a database is very wide. Moreover, there is the database as a whole and its individual components, such as names and addresses in a telephone directory. If the database comprises a collection of songs, then the individual components themselves will be copyright works. However, where the database lists names only, those names are not in themselves protected by copyright because – as we saw in the Exxon case in Chapter 2 – names are too short to get copyright protection in their own right.

Drawing from the contents of a database or a substantial part of it, whether in one go or gradually, such as by systematically taking insubstantial parts over a period of time, will be an infringement of database right if not undertaken with the permission of the owner of the database. The owner of the database right will be the person who has created the database or invested time and resources in producing the database.

Before extracting names and addresses from a database, consider whether you would be infringing on database rights. Many databases will incorporate some material, such as a fictitious name and address, that is purely designed to alert the owner of your use of the database.

Although a database right lasts only 15 years, it can last indefinitely if the database is substantially changed during the 15-year period, including from the 'accumulation of successive additions, deletions, or alterations which would result in the database being considered to be a substantial new investment'.

Anyone creating, organising or administering databases – or extracting and reusing the contents of databases belonging to others – should review their position. Among other things, if you are creating a database, make sure you keep a record of the 'financial, human or technical resources' you put into the database as proof of substantial investment. Keep a separate record of any investment you make in the organisation and arrangement of the database itself in addition to any investment in the creation of the data.

Complying with regulations affecting websites

Regulations mean that your site should be accessible to those with disabilities so it is usable for the blind or the deaf. You must also carefully control access to any information that you process. You will need an appropriate privacy policy in order to meet your data protection obligations.

Websites commonly aim to persuade visitors to leave their contact details so they can stay in touch with their users. Capturing such data in your database and sending newsletters and occasional emails to the contacts in your list may result in the visitor eventually buying something from you.

Bear in mind that you might decide to sell the business in the future, so make sure your database is properly collected and maintained. Part of this obligation will involve getting appropriate consents and keeping a record of them, so that if, for example, you share contact details with third parties you can show that you comply with data protection regulations and have the relevant consents to do so.

You would comply with these regulations by having a privacy policy that mentions how personal details are going to be used by your company, what cookies are on your site, and how people may withdraw their consent. For example, if you recorded video at any events you held, you might show footage that features individuals filmed at such events. It would be good practice to explain this in your privacy policy. It may also be wise to suggest that people do not attend your events if they are not willing to give their consent to their image being used in this way.

Although data protection and related legislation may set the threshold of what is acceptable in relation to email marketing, your contract with your email service provider may have even more stringent clauses.

Some hosting companies may be contractually entitled to seek damages from customers engaged in unsolicited bulk mail. As a rule of thumb, therefore, the terms of business from a hosting service should always be reviewed before engaging in direct marketing.

Complying with legal requirements is explained in the Appendix..

Gavin's products – video courses

At TTMC, Gavin has a range of products he intends to sell via an e-commerce store on his website. For example, his speaking engagements have become a significant source of income in the last six months or so. So, in a bid to find an efficient way to scale delivery of his expertise without needing to be in two places at once, he has come up with the idea of recording and packaging his talks for delivery on DVDs and also as downloads.

Some of these will be packaged with a service element, while others will be sold as products on their own, and one of the videos will be offered freely via his YouTube channel, although he also wants it embedded in his website.

Gavin needs to understand about the Distance Selling Regulations and the Electronic Commerce Regulations, and how they impact on the design of his website and his terms of business. In particular, he should ensure that prospective buyers are supplied with a variety of information, including contact details, VAT and company registration information.

Gavin must also ensure that he is able to supply his terms of business in durable form, rather than just on a web page in his e-store. He could satisfy this legal requirement by sending a PDF via email, although it would also be a good idea to attach a PDF version of the terms on his web page to ensure he complies with the regulations at the point of sale.

It's also important for Gavin to structure the purchase transactions carefully. Specifically, placing an order through his website should not be enough to conclude a contract. This is essential, in case there are pricing errors on the website. He should only be bound contractually when he has approved an order. Even the most diligent companies make expensive mistakes. Many instances of price errors have been widely publicised, including that of Kodak in 2002, when it had to honour 2,000 orders for a £329 digital camera listed at the erroneously low price of £100.

Some of Gavin's customers may be interested in buying boxed sets of the videos at a premium, so his returns policy on his website, which must comply with statutory requirements regarding refunds, should discuss who pays for postage, in what condition videos must be returned, and the limits of the right.

Conclusion

Gavin realises that there are a number of issues to consider when commissioning his website. Marketing and other considerations have an impact on the type of website he might commission and the content he may want to allow links for.

Chapter 6: Key take-home messages

■ Before commissioning a website, be clear about how you will market online and what you expect from your website.

■ Get a specification drawn up and then get like-for-like quotes.

■ Have the contract reviewed.

■ Discuss online branding and your name and domain name choice with your lawyer.

■ Before taking delivery of the site and making a final payment, it's important to have your lawyer check the site to ensure it does not infringe on third party rights and that it complies with regulations.

Part Three

Brand Promotion

Chapter 7

Copyright in the 'cloud' – how the Internet impacts on copyright

'If you reveal your secrets to the wind, you should not blame the wind for revealing them to the trees' Kahlil Gibran

We know that an important factor in achieving success online involves having a site that appears more prominently than your competitors' sites when potential customers are searching for your products or services.

The bottom line on the Internet is that people are looking for information. Having lots of freely available good content is the route to online success. SEO benefits will kick in from links to your content, and your site will be ranked more prominently in the search engines.

A rule of thumb for online business success could involve giving away as much as 80% of the value you have to offer, in order to encourage 20% of users to buy additional information or services from you. This 'freemium' model of Internet business is challenging industries such as law and news organisations which generally charge for information.

New business models are being sought to support the giving away of so much information for free, and many businesses are extremely worried that competitors will copy their content. In this environment, it helps if you are clear about the limits of copyright – what it does and doesn't protect and, consequently, what material you might want to avoid putting online, bearing in mind the available remedies if your material were copied. Possibly it is even more important to understand the dynamics of publishing material that your competitors could gain insights from, and then exploit, before you were ready to benefit from your own ideas.

We'll look at the extent to which copyright protects your ideas in the next chapter as well as the implications of releasing material early. For now, let's concentrate on the issues surrounding copyright online and what options are available for tackling copyright infringement.

What copyright protects

If you are in the news business, it's important for any news stories you source to be credited to you. If you scooped an important piece of news, and that story was picked up (though not copied) by another, more prominent website, then that website would be widely credited as the initiator of the story. So, as well as releasing the piece of news, you might want to publicise the fact that you were the source of that story by issuing a PR web press release. Don't assume people will know the story came from you. It's also doubly important to focus on getting good search engine rankings.

In fact, it may sometimes be advisable NOT to put certain content online – particularly in view of the fast-changing nature of technologies that facilitate copying.

Digital rights management

Digital rights management (DRM) schemes comprise a wide range of techniques used to restrict the use of hardware, software and media, in order to allow publishers broad control over how the software is used by licensees.

Piracy of films and music has been around for years. With the introduction of eReaders such as the Kindle and the iPad, eBook piracy has also become a problem. Previously, it was difficult to produce a pirated book online. It was necessary to have the original files and find someone with enough time to scan the book onto a computer. In contrast, copying eBooks is a much simpler task as they are already in digital form.

So far, the tactics employed by publishing companies include the use of DRM, delaying electronic editions of their books, or simply refusing to make their books available in digital form. With the introduction of digital music purchases came the rise of DRM, restricting how the music that was purchased could be used.

With traditional media, music was generally freely playable and transferable, but the past decade has seen increasing restrictions imposed on consumers, controlling which portable device the music is played on, how many computers it can be used on, and how long you have access to it.

DRM has proved unsuccessful in the music industry as it hasn't been effective in preventing people from producing pirated copies of files.

Game publishers are increasingly making use of these schemes in their attempts to combat video game piracy but, arguably, this only serves to aggravate people who have purchased files legally.

Case study: Newspaper Licensing Agency Ltd

A controversial case, *Newspaper Licensing Agency Ltd v. Meltwater*, has tested the courts' ability to do justice between the parties without causing jurisprudential problems in the law.

Meltwater is a news monitoring service and news aggregator providing an electronic press cuttings service via email and a website for PR agencies interested in being alerted when their clients are in the news. It holds a web end user licence (WEUL) to provide the service.

In the offline world, such a news aggregator would be a news cutting service, which sends news clippings featuring clients to the PR agencies.

These news aggregation sites pay a licence fee as they would if they were a news cuttings service. However, the decision concerned also charging their users – the PR agencies – a licence fee for clicking on the links sent by the news aggregator.

In determining that fees be charged for clicking on the links, the court has upset a balance that previously existed in various aspects of the law. For example, due to the way computers function, every time we visit a web page our computers make a copy of it. This means we are technically infringing copyright. This technical infringement problem was solved by legislation enacted in section 28A of the copyright legislation, which provided that merely incidental copying was exempt from copyright infringement. So, surfing on the web and linking to content does not constitute copyright infringement.

The basis of this law was upset by the *Meltwater* decision that clicking on the link to read a news item did not fall within the exceptions for temporary or transient copies. On the contrary, the court thought that the process of displaying a web page on a computer is only exempted from copyright infringement if there is 'lawful' use of the work. The court decided that lawful means that permission has been given. Therefore if a publisher has not given permission, there is breach of copyright when PR agencies click to read the news story sent to them by Meltwater.

The case is currently awaiting the decision of the Court of Appeal. Decisions reached in the lower courts have shown the tensions that arise when the law tries to reconcile legal questions in a way that protects the economic interests of an industry (in this case, the newspaper industry) but which causes problems for the Internet as a whole.

The ruling affects most (if not all) businesses subscribing to a media monitoring service that contains content from online newspapers. Free aggregators like Google News will not be affected by this ruling. But the upshot of the decision is that although *Meltwater* does not affect surfers' ability to browse the Internet without fear of infringing copyright, it will sometimes be unclear whether or not the clicking will be lawful, and as such the ruling has left the law in an untidy state which needs clarification.

In the meantime, small business owners like Gavin need clarification on what they can and can't do, and what they might realistically do to protect their intellectual property.

DRM for small businesses?

Gavin had queried whether digital rights management (DRM) software might be the way to prevent copying of the DVDs and other copyright material he intends to sell. As he intends to release valuable content on his website in order to get links and SEO success, he wonders how to prevent website visitors copying and pasting his web pages.

Technical approaches may not be the solution to the problems of copying due to the drawbacks of DRM software. For instance, DRM software could have an adverse impact on your search engine rankings and alienate visitors to your website by making your website less user-friendly, and you are still faced with the problem of users finding ways of getting round this if they are determined to copy your content.

Trying to prevent copying through DRM software is unpopular among consumers in many industries. These techniques have not resolved the problems of copyright infringement for larger, well-resourced companies. This is despite the music industry being vocal in its condemnation of illegal music downloading. Smaller businesses are therefore unlikely to find it any easier to enforce their rights and prevent copying by adopting DRM.

Far better, before publishing content online, is to carefully evaluate what the consequences might be for your business if someone copied a particular piece of content, either word for word, or by using the ideas incorporated within it.

While word-for-word copying of a substantial part of your content would amount to copyright infringement, it's possible that someone can get round this by putting your ideas into their own words.

Let's take a look at what might happen if your content is 'scraped'.

Content scraping

Content 'scraping' occurs when someone takes content from your site without permission, and uses a copy of it on their own site, often claiming they wrote it.

Search engines have still not figured out how to block sites that scrape content from their search results, so content-scrapers can populate a web page with other people's content and then use that content to attract traffic. They tend to sell ads and, in some cases, infect visitors with malware. Sometimes more wholesale copying happens, whereby a 'mirror' site is set up, copying all the content of a site.

There are some steps you can take to find out if your content is being scraped, such as setting up a link back to your website so that if the whole article is taken you can use the backlink analysis to track down copiers. This involves either using specialist tools or delivering special instructions to search engines to find websites that link to you. Another approach is to set up Google Alerts so you receive an email when the search engine finds a web page containing your content. Services like copyscape.com are also useful for identifying whether other sites have copied your material. Of course, these techniques do not prevent copying, but they do help you to track down perpetrators.

Internet Protocol addresses

In practice, an effective way to keep content scrapers from accessing your content is if you know the potential infringer's Internet Protocol (IP) address. You may then ban it from your website. However, if they are determined to scrape your content, this may not have a lasting impact as they can change their IP address.

So there is no sure-fire way of picking the culprit out of every individual visitor. A key difficulty in protecting your content is that it can have a negative impact on the usability of your website for your other visitors.

Having a website that ranks highly in search results at least gives you the comfort of appearing more prominently than sites that scraped your content.

While in some cases if someone has actually copied your content in an infringing way (i.e. word for word), legal action may be an appropriate way forward, it is not necessarily the only option.

Cooks Source, highlighted later in this chapter is an example of how copying content can come back to haunt a business, and how an author can obtain all the justice they could have hoped for without need for litigation.

Disregard for copyright online

One aspect of online business that is particularly difficult to grapple with is copyright. It is your responsibility as site owner to ensure you are not infringing on third party rights when using content.

Newcomers to the Internet freely copy and paste from other websites, whether there is a copyright notice on the site or not, but particularly if there is no copyright notice. They assume they can use any work they like on the Internet, or that the lack of a copyright notice means the work is in the public domain.

Although the strict letter of copyright law is not always observed or enforced on the Internet, you still need to be aware of what is protected by copyright, and what you may or may not do with other people's copyright works. Sometimes, to protect your copyright you may first need to find out the identity of the person who used it. If they downloaded your eBook by leaving an anonymous email address and have since infringed your copyright in the eBook, you first have to establish their identity. You could do this by reference to their IP address, as discussed in Chapter 8, which explains the problems of anonymity generally and the available remedies open to tackling it.

Rights holders whose rights are infringed in the UK inevitably need to concern themselves with these wider issues including the Digital Economy Act.

Digital Economy Act

The Digital Economy Act 2010 (DEA), which aims to strike a balance between the interests of the public and the interests of the creative industry in enforcing their copyright online, provides a framework that includes a mechanism for the Secretary of State for Culture, Media and Sport (DCMS) to block access to websites that contribute to copyright infringement. It also allows for disconnection of repeat infringers.

Under the scheme, Internet providers were recently due to begin sending out warning letters to customers who are the subject of complaints by copyright owners. However, following controversy over the impact of the new rules some telecoms companies applied for judicial review of the Act, which has delayed its impact.

The Court of Appeal dismissed objections to the Act brought by BT and TalkTalk, and concluded that it was proportionate in the way it deals with infringement online, and that the increased costs to Internet service providers (ISPs) were justified. Still, this is by no means the end of the process.

Three issues in particular will see the full impact of the Act delayed for quite some time. Firstly, the DCMS observed that further review of cost-sharing legislation is necessary. This follows a ruling that ISPs ought not to have to bear responsibility for 25% of the cost of handling appeals from customers who receive copyright infringement warnings. Secondly, the initial draft code produced by Ofcom, setting out ISPs' obligations under the law, is expected to see a second revision after deficiencies in the cost-sharing legislation have been addressed. Thirdly, technical measures to disconnect or limit access to the Internet by copyright infringers are not likely to be deployed until at least a year later, after users begin to receive notification that their connections are being used for infringement.

In addition to these delays, the eventual impact of the Act has been called into question following recent disputes over the blocking of websites used for infringement.

Case study: Newzbin

Newzbin, and its successor, Newzbin2, were web-based services allowing users to search for mentions of material like music, films, and software, much of which was protected by copyright. While the search results by themselves were often of little use, users paying a subscription had access to information about where they could actually download the files, and the service turned a significant profit.

However, both were eventually found by the courts to have contributed to copyright infringement. Newzbin went into liquidation following legal action in 2010. Later, having resurfaced in the Seychelles as Newzbin2, the UK High Court ordered major ISPs to block access to the site.

More recently, the Pirate Bay, a website offering for free a service not unlike that of Newzbin, was found to have sanctioned, approved and countenanced copyright infringement by its users, and was subjected to a similar blocking order.

To some extent these decisions broke new ground, as the sites didn't actually host copyright material themselves, just information about where to find it. They did, however, go somewhat further than this, and were held to have encouraged infringement by their users. This doesn't mean you can sleep easy if you avoid actively promoting copyright infringement. If visitors share information through your site, it's important to be aware that you, rather than your users, may find yourself the first target of legal action relating to any infringement.

Certain regulations can protect you from liability if you are unaware of the activity, and avoid taking an active role in moderating user content, but relying on these exemptions is a risky strategy. Once you are aware, or should be aware that a service you offer is being used for infringement, you are likely to find these exemptions no longer apply.

What the Newzbin cases highlight is the increasing propensity of copyright owners to enforce their rights online. In fact, the government has decided that existing legislation offers enough scope for blocking infringing websites, and so for the moment does not intend to implement the blocking provided for by the Digital Economy Act.

So, for now it's unclear how effective the Act will be in practice and, until publication of the expected second draft of Ofcom's code of obligations, it's difficult even to accurately predict what recourse copyright owners will have for infringement. Despite this, some commentators suggest the Act is already outdated and will not do enough to discourage piracy.

Conjecture aside, what does seem clear is that we are likely to see a system allowing copyright owners to notify ISPs of infringements of their copyright online. As notifications against the same individual or organisation build up, eventually reaching a certain threshold, we expect to see ISPs taking action to limit their users' access to the Internet.

How will the DEA affect business owners?

Well, if your business relies on Internet access (which business doesn't nowadays?), it is crucial that you guard against online copyright infringement by your employees, and the way to do this is to develop a well-thought-out Internet policy to educate staff and freelancers working for you. Failing to do so has the potential to bring your business to a halt if you are cut off by your ISP.

An Internet policy is essential to handle these and other risks for your brand.

On the other side of the coin, for vigilant businesses the Act could offer a more cost-effective way to curb copyright infringement. Before the new legislation, the IP address of an Internet connection used to infringe your copyright was not enough information to take action; it was first necessary to apply to the court to unmask the owner of that Internet connection. While under the new regime a court order will still be necessary to identify the owner of a connection, notifications will allow copyright owners, at least indirectly, to warn them against infringement.

With the Act potentially introducing both risks and opportunities into the equation, one very valid concern is that false accusations could damage your reputation. Some of the techniques used to identify copyright infringers online have led to controversy, and while lawyers have borne the brunt of the backlash to widespread legal threats, over zealous use of these new notification mechanisms could lead to consumer resentment.

Tracking online copyright infringement can lead to false positives, and sending warnings to innocent users is not likely to go unnoticed.

Taking steps to ensure you do not infringe the copyright of others is as important as protecting your own copyright. A case which shows how social media and the Internet is impacting law enforcement in surprising ways which could have a considerable impact on a business, was *Cooks Source*.

The Cooks Source

The *Cooks Source* magazine was shut down due to the disapproval of the online community when the magazine's editor, instead of apologising for using material by blogger Monica Gaudio without her permission, justified its use by saying:

The web is considered 'public domain' and you should be happy we just didn't 'lift' your whole article and put someone else's name on it! It happens a lot, clearly more than you are aware of, especially on college campuses, and the workplace. If you took offence and are unhappy, I am sorry, but you as a professional should know that the article we used written by you was in very bad need of editing, and is much better now than was originally.

This response was so astonishing that it went viral, and the backlash of the online community was incredible. Songs were written, websites set up, and campaigns set in motion. Mainstream media, including the *Guardian*, picked up the story and in a matter of weeks the magazine had shut down completely.

What is clear is that the Internet is developing rapidly and making subtle changes to the way we live and interact. These developments combine to create threats and opportunities that are very profound.

Conclusion

As copyright infringement on the Internet is a reality, it's important to be prepared for this environment. Consider carefully what to feature online. Be alert to competitors getting wind of your ideas too soon before you've had a chance to implement them.

Chapter 7: Key take-home messages

■ Before publishing content online, evaluate what the consequences might be for your business if someone copied your content.

■ Consider using measures like backlink, Google Alerts or copyscape.com to help you track down people who copy your site's content.

■ If you know the Internet Protocol (IP) address of a copyright infringer, you can ban them from using your website, although they could still get round this by changing their IP address.

■ Develop an Internet policy on copyright infringement to educate staff and freelancers working for you.

Chapter 8

How intellectual property law protects your ideas

'Don't worry about people stealing your ideas. If your ideas are any good, you'll have to ram them down people's throats' Howard Aiken

Copying is so rife in business that if you have a profitable niche or concept, it would be naive to believe that competitors won't sooner or later try to capture some of your market share.

Competitors will be keeping an eye out and will copy those elements of your business that they believe to be effective. However, what if someone crosses the bounds of acceptable, legitimate competition and engages in unethical practices? How does the law help if someone crosses the bounds of what seems acceptable?

In this chapter we'll look at the extent to which intellectual property laws can help when competitors copy your ideas. Whether they are copying your ideas, or using a similar name to yours in order to divert business away from you to themselves, the question turns on what is acceptable and unacceptable copying, and how a business might protect itself.

Competition

It's only sensible to expect imitators if you come up with an innovative idea, as Seth Godin explains in *Purple Cow* (Penguin Books, 2003): 'Why do birds fly in formation? Because the birds that follow the leader have an easier flight. The leader breaks the wind resistance, and the following birds can fly far more efficiently'.

So if you demonstrate a breakthrough idea, and others can see that it's a good one, they will copy it. They will benefit from the fact that you've shown them the way forward.

As Jack Trout explains in *Differentiate or Die* (John Wiley & Sons, 2000), being first, even if you hang around for a while, is still no guarantee of success. For example, Leica was the technology and market leader for decades in 35mm cameras until the Japanese copied German technology, improved on it, and then lowered the prices. The pioneer failed to react and ended up a bit player.

However, not all copying is tolerated by the law, and copyright may sometimes be used to stop the theft of intellectual property. At other times, different IP rights may be more powerful in stopping whatever it is the copyists are doing.

In Chapter 5 I explained how different IP rights provide different kinds of protection over the same brand elements or products. The way to have strong IP protection in your business is to secure as many of these IP rights as possible for each element of your brand or product, because each right will protect you in subtly different ways and situations.

Just as armies going to war would take an array of artillery with them, such as hand grenades, rifles and guns, in order to have an appropriate weapon at their disposal for the various scenarios they might encounter, so it is with IP rights. You want to have a range of rights to rely on so that you can use the most appropriate ones, depending on the situation that might arise.

It's worth mentioning that the attitudes within present-day society do not favour an overly protectionist approach towards intellectual property. There is a climate of abundance, collaboration and sharing online which makes it decidedly 'uncool' to be pedantic about copyright and other IP rights. Instead of keeping your ideas tightly under your own control, the prevailing philosophy is to publish and spread your ideas in order to profit from them.

It is perfectly possible, and sensible even, not to be too hung up about protecting your intellectual property and still make sensible business decisions such as ensuring you own the rights in products you are creating for your business. The point of doing so is to avoid having someone put a stop to your sales, and claim damages and an account of profits for infringing on their rights. You should adopt the same matter-of-fact approach to owning IP rights and avoiding IP infringement as you would when buying insurance to protect you in case your property burnt down. It's not really about whether some disaster might befall you and why and how.

Because we are in the relatively early days of the knowledge economy, the legal concepts for how to go about securing ownership of intangibles are not well understood, and there's much misinformation spread around.

Gavin, from our example business TTMC, intends to own the rights in his products, and wants to know how to protect his business against damaging copying by competitors. He is not aiming to stop every technical breach of his IP right that he encounters.

He has a plan to provide the service element of his offering by licensing businesses in other countries to deliver his methodology. His planned range of products will be sold globally via his e-commerce store. Apart from eBooks and various courses, he intends to deliver his methodology through video courses and an app.

TTMC time-saver app

Gavin has published an app before and engaged an IT business to develop a basic tool that allowed people to buy and watch his videos online. The app was published through the App Store, but things fell apart.

First of all, the developers went out of business and Gavin couldn't track them down to have a new feature implemented. Worse still, the app was taken offline when it was found not to comply with the store guidelines, because it allowed users to pay Gavin directly to watch videos, rather than using approved mechanisms which gave Apple a cut of the revenue. Gavin later discovered that his developer had handed all of the app source code to another business before closing down, and this business had used it to release a similar product.

After taking legal advice to determine whether he could claim a stake in their profits, or at least ask for a copy of the source code, Gavin discovered that his contract with the developer had not dealt appropriately with copyright ownership. Although he had a licence to use and sell the software, he was not the copyright owner and could neither demand a copy of the source code nor of the revenue from their use of it.

Gavin now plans to package some of his expertise and experience in an app for mobile devices, aimed at helping company directors to make more constructive use of their time. He's spotted the popularity of similar software on the Apple and Android marketplaces. His proposed app would include a task list, diary, notes on time management, and video refresher courses covering some of the more universal topics that Gavin focuses on when consulting.

Having learnt from his mistakes, Gavin's approach with the new app will be radically different. Gavin consulted IP lawyers early on, once he'd found developers willing to offer ownership of the copyright, and so a software development contract was produced for him to use to ensure that the project went to plan. The contract provided appropriate safeguards, including a software escrow arrangement offering protection against losing the source code if the developers went under, as well as a clause allowing him to withhold payment if the app did not meet the requirements of major retailers.

Gavin realises he could learn more about his users by collecting details about the way they manage their time, so he asked for the app to include a mechanism for collecting and then aggregating the data, intending to use this information to offer better services in future. He let his lawyers know about his plans in advance, and he was advised from a data protection perspective before he spent more money on the development. As a result, he decided to make some adjustments to increase the privacy of users and discussed these with the developers. He also had drafted, an appropriate privacy policy informing users how their information would be used.

How does copyright prevent copying of ideas?

As a general rule, as discussed in Chapter 5, copyright protects the expression of an idea – namely, the actual words used – rather than the underlying idea. So, if someone put your material into their own words, with minimal word-for-word copying, it might be difficult to establish copyright infringement.

As for the ideas incorporated in a piece of writing, film or music CD, it would be difficult to stop others borrowing from your ideas and communicating them in their own words. Copyright law cannot be used as a tool to stop your competitors setting up a similar line of business. So, writing down your business ideas will not stop competitors from using those ideas.

Only a patent can give you a monopoly over ideas (assuming those ideas take the form of a product or system that is capable of being patented).

Sharing your skills and ideas

Think carefully before revealing knowledge or offering up your best ideas online. Pause to consider whether your competitors might get an unfair advantage by knowing this information. Could it be that releasing your ideas too soon might give others the opportunity to beat you to the punch?

Being smart about how and when and whether to release know-how and ideas is the way to benefit from disseminating your ideas. You want to get exposure without seriously disadvantaging yourself.

Generally, this means allowing sufficient lead time to bring your ideas to fruition before revealing them.

Early promotion may be useful to drum up interest, but if you misjudge the timing you could simply give competitors your good idea and miss an opportunity to lead the market if they were to run with your idea before you had a chance to implement and develop it. On the other hand, it's important to be realistic about what competitors could or might do, and in what timescales. Only you can be the judge of what to publish and when, but you need to temper your fears with a large dose of realism.

When could you object to someone copying your ideas?

While copyright does not always prevent others using ideas embodied in your materials, there are some forms of copying which, though not word-for-word copying, could nevertheless amount to infringement of your copyright.

For example, if someone was giving a lecture and you copied the lecture word for word by recording it, and then used the material in a competing business, it's likely the speaker could validly object to this theft of their content because of the initial infringement of copyright (the speaker's performance rights would have been infringed by your recording). Similarly, if you take so much detail from a work so that it could be argued you had copied a substantial part of it, you would have difficulty in justifying your copying.

Copying by creating script

In Chapter 5, we looked at the case of *Hodgson and Jarvie v. Isaac and Notting Hill Movies* (2011) and how a film script based on a book amounted to copying a substantial part of the book without permission, even though there was no copying of words.

Because of the complexity of copyright law and people's desire to stay on the right side of the law, avoiding copyright infringement is an incentive for most people not to copy competitors' materials too much. So, if the details of Gavin's time management solutions were copied, he might be able to take action. However, it wouldn't be possible to prevent others copying his ideas about the importance of managing your affairs so as to reduce your inbox daily, or how to use software tools to manage your information overload.

Despite the theoretical copyright infringement if too much detail is taken from others' ideas, just pause to consider the diet industry. There are so many diets that borrow from the Atkins diet and put their own spin on it, that it's obviously not possible to prevent others running with your best ideas and improving them. I've come across diets that slavishly copy details of Timothy Ferriss's *The 4-Hour Body* (Ebury Publishing, 2011), applying their own name and branding to it. It's possible that some of them even come too close and fall on the wrong side of copying. However, as long as they are not using Tim Ferriss's name, or referring to their solutions as 'The 4-Hour Body' (that is borrowing from his goodwill), they are unlikely to be pursued for copyright infringement. To some extent, that might be because Tim Ferriss is so successful that these copyists would not come on his radar as being a cause for concern. So, another important principle about IP infringement is the surrounding circumstances – who is copying whom, and whether anyone would object.

That's why you must know when to publish your ideas, and be ready to profit from the publication by having products and services in place to meet the demand that your ideas may generate. You need to keep improving and staying ahead of the competition and become better known than them.

In terms of our example business, TTMC, although Gavin has already published a book, his best ideas are still in his head. He plans to publish a second book, which he anticipates will see his business blossom. He expects to have applications from consultants worldwide who want to become approved practitioners of his methods.

Do trade marks prevent copying of your process, method or system?

While it is not possible to trade-mark a business method, process or system, trade marks can indirectly protect a business's processes, methods or system.

When a trade mark becomes associated in consumers' minds with your activity, then the fact that the brand name is how people identify and associate with your activity gives you powerful rights. They have no other way of getting the benefits of what your brand sells except to use its name.

That's how Anywayup Cup had protection through its brand name, and how Zumba has a monopoly on its dance fitness programme. The dance itself could possibly be recreated by someone else (indeed dancers say that the Zumba dance itself comprises existing dance routines introduced by other choreographers), but the end result could not be called Zumba. Nor could a competitor use a name similar to Zumba in order to piggyback on its success, without infringing on its trade mark.

What about copying someone's business? For example, it is acceptable to copy Ikea's idea of selling its furniture using a self-service system whereby customers go round the warehouse, pick out what they want, and wheel items to the checkout desk to pay. However, the law would intervene if someone either pretended to be Ikea by using a similar name or used distinctive elements of its 'trade dress' (see below).

Trade dress

'Trade dress' refers to all the different ways in which a brand's visual identity is manifested. To explain how a 'trade dress' infringement might arise, let's take Starbucks as an example.

Starbucks has a distinctive method of doing business, which is recognised and protected in large part by its name, logo and visual designs. Its methods of doing business are able to be freely copied in the same way as Ikea's are – namely, in the case of Starbucks, a coffee house using baristas where you give your order, receive your coffee and if you're drinking it indoors, you can do so relaxing in sofas and chairs in comfortable surroundings. Coffee Republic, Mocha and countless other coffee shop chains were able to flourish by following Starbucks' lead. But if another coffee shop used a name reminiscent of Starbucks – such as STARBOK – it would be infringing Starbucks' trade mark rights.

If this business also copied Starbucks' decor by using a combination of the Starbucks interior design features, colour combinations, and a similar logo it would risk crossing the boundary of acceptable competition. A 'passing off' action would be the way to protect the 'get-up' of the premises. (See Chapter 15 for more about 'passing off'.)

Keeping ideas to yourself

It's generally sensible to keep your cards close to your chest if you have a great idea for a name – for a product, a new business concept which is easily copied or a new book. Once you tell others, there is a risk that a third party may beat you to the punch, for example, by applying to register the name as a trade mark before you get to do so, as happened to Kalaxia in Chapter 2. For similar reasons, if you have stumbled upon some innovative way to sell a product or service that your competitors have yet to work out, it makes sense to advise staff not to discuss it with their friends when they're down the pub. Staff may not realise how sensitive the information is if you don't point it out to them. If you don't want to see someone else take your idea and implement it before you've had a chance to do so, keep it quiet.

Such copying can be a serious concern if you've spotted a gap in the market for something and don't want to alert a competitor to it. Usually, businesses are busy with their own projects and plans, and it takes time for larger ones to get approval to move forward with new ones. So, think about the practicalities involved, as well as what you uniquely bring to the idea give you a competitive edge, even if a competitor copied your idea.

Often it's how an idea is implemented, rather than the idea itself, that determines how well it is received in the market. For example, search engines were in widespread use when Google entered the market and stole market share with its unique approach to improving the experience of surfers.

When in doubt, talk to an IP lawyer if you are concerned that revealing your ideas to others prematurely could have damaging consequences for you, such as potentially losing you the chance to patent an idea. If you have a patentable idea, then you should generally file a patent application before discussing its details with third parties, whether or not they sign a confidentiality agreement. Non-disclosure agreements (i.e. confidentiality agreements) are common when discussing business concepts with third parties like web designers. But don't take too much comfort from the mere signing of a confidentiality agreement. Not all situations merit the same type of non-disclosure agreement (NDA). Some projects would entail including appropriate restrictions in your contracts with others, not just a requirement to maintain confidentiality. For example, you may want to restrict your web designer from outsourcing the major part of the work on Elance or other platforms.

Potential investors

It's unlikely that potential investors would be willing to sign non-disclosure agreements. It's more to your advantage that they hear what you have to say than it is to theirs. That's because, statistically, there are a lot more people looking for investment than there are investors.

In any event, if your idea is patentable, even if an investor would be willing to sign a non-disclosure agreement, the right step is to first file the patent application as mentioned earlier. Investors would expect you to have protected your idea in this way as it shows professionalism as well as belief in yourself and your invention. It illustrates that you're willing to put up some of your own money in pursuit of your idea.

It's difficult to raise funds for a mere idea, because an idea is not enough to carry a business from nothing to success. An idea is the starting point that all great things are based upon. However, it's unlikely to attract investment until some progress has been made implementing it.

Ideas v. implementation

Seasoned business owners know that it's not the idea that creates success so much as how that idea is given life and implemented. The first to market tends to make the mistakes that subsequent entrants into the market learn from and avoid.

Given that people will copy good ideas, when planning a new business or product launch it's important to consider how easily replicable the business concept might be. Do you have a unique business model? If so, how easy would it be for competitors to copy it? What are the 'barriers to entry' into your market?

For example, Gavin's ideas for a web-based time management training platform would have a higher barrier to entry than a similar social media training platform. Social media is relatively new, while time management has a longer history of knowledge behind it. This knowledge tends to be confined to a smaller group of professionals, and any writings that exist on the topic are difficult for laypeople to digest as they are written for academic research. Time management is therefore accessible to fewer people, so if you have a brilliant idea for a time management solution it's less likely to lead to someone else rushing off to implement it before you do, than an idea relating to an area such as social media, which is more widely understood and sought after. On the other hand, the market for social media training will be wider.

Consider who would be a threat if they entered the same market as the one you've created. If your idea is unique, you will have a 'first mover' advantage over competitors and so get a few months' lead time. Is that lead time going to be enough to give you a sustained advantage? Bear in mind the resources you have compared to those of your competitors.

If your competitor is an international conglomerate with deep pockets and your idea is for a product that's not patentable, how would you be able to fight off such competition? It's not worth creating a market for something that you don't own the rights over, and the experience of Mandy Haberman, inventor of the Anywayup Cup, illustrates this point. She has publicly said:

Because I had patents, I was able to go to court, defend my idea, enforce my patent rights and that meant that I kept my monopoly in the market. This made me a lot of money; if I had not had the patents, I would not have made anything.

In practice, patent protection is critical to success for many types of product-based business ideas where larger, well-resourced manufacturers would present a threat if they decided to enter that market.

Therefore, Gavin's idea for a time management desk product that might be patented is unlikely to be worth pursuing further unless he is willing to file a patent application for it, as well as protect its visual features with a design application.

The inventor of the Karaoke machine, Daisuke Inoue, earned nothing from the billion-dollar industry that the invention spawned. He never thought of patenting his invention until it was too late and, by then, he had lost millions potentially. Reflecting on his experience, one can't help feel it's not fair that it was the multinationals and not him who made massive financial gains from his invention. However, his case is not unusual and, even now, many inventors know little about their intellectual property rights.

Confidentiality is key to patentability

Talking about the details of your invention before you've protected it with a patent is something to be avoided as it will jeopardise your chances of securing a patent over your innovation. If you haven't thought to protect your idea this way, then once you've disclosed your idea, it's 'out there' and it will be too late to secure a patent. Always adopt a policy of not discussing your ideas with others until you've taken advice.

As mentioned, if you do have an invention that you know is patentable, file a patent application before you discuss it with any potential investors.

When deciding whether to file for patent protection, bear in mind that patents can be expensive to maintain. Just because you can patent an innovation does not mean it is necessarily a good idea to do so. However, having a patent pending application over an innovation can be a useful way of warding off competition for 12 months. The details of your application do not become public until 18 months after you filed the application. At that stage, the details of your patent application are published, so competitors will then be in a position to assess the quality of your patent, and design around it, if they can find a way to do so.

One approach that works well for many inventors is to file the initial application so you get patent pending status. The cost of this is relatively modest compared to the costs down the line, which can mount considerably. Then use the 12-month patent pending period to assess whether it's worth proceeding further with the application. If it's not, then you could abandon the application on expiry of the 12-month period.

Earlier I discussed how IP rights such as trade marks might indirectly protect a 'process', 'method' or 'system' of doing business. But you can't register a business process patent in the UK, although it might be possible in the US. However, you could begin a patent application in the UK that you know will ultimately only be capable of becoming a patent in the US. You would then benefit from the more affordable and accessible prices of UK patent attorneys to start the application process.

Example US Business Process Patent – Amazon's 1-Click patent

Amazon's famous '1-Click' system for online orders is an example of how the US sometimes grants business process patents, such as in the case of software patents.

Amazon's innovation consisted of a way of allowing online shoppers to buy products with a single click. Instead of entering payment details each time, the Amazon servers identify visitors using a cookie stored on their computer and retrieve the information automatically. Amazon secured patent protection for the technique in the US back in September 1999. However, its efforts to obtain protection from the European Patent Office have been unsuccessful, owing to the differences in the treatment of applications for patent protection of software within Europe.

Every non-trivial piece of software involves a series of technical problems overcome through the innovative application of a developer's expertise and experience. Code is written and problems are overcome daily by software engineers worldwide. The 1-Click 'innovation' by Amazon is far from the most complex of these.

The UK's approach to software patents

While patents offer an important incentive to innovate, and a just reward to those who develop new technology benefiting society, the way the UK patent system approaches software patents is to avoid setting the bar for patent protection too low. Otherwise, the fear is that smaller players in the software field who cannot afford to acquire patent portfolios of software or to pay for licensing agreements, may be forced out of the market altogether.

When considering patenting, keep in mind that patents, particularly software-based ones, are potentially rife with infringement litigation, especially within the US. This can make it particularly difficult for a small company to decide whether to spend what might be a huge proportion of its IP budget on patent protection when other elements of its IP, such as its brand, have yet to be secured. As the brand is a very powerful way to indirectly protect a business's processes or methods it may well represent better use of a company's resources to protect that.

Another factor to take into account with patents is that certain companies hold portfolios of patents with the pure objective of enforcing their rights against purported infringers, and sometimes even against non-copiers.

Enforcement of patents is their business rather than manufacturing or research, and the objective is to collect royalty income from their portfolios. As the cost of defending against a patent infringement suit is extremely high, you have the problem of facing potentially expensive litigation or settlement terms, even if you were not infringing and would be successful in court. Litigation always has an inherent uncertainty and unpredictability, which makes any potential litigation a serious concern for any but the most affluent of businesses.

Even where a patent would be available, think of the experience of inventors such as Mandy Haberman and James Dyson, who had to devote considerable time and resources to protecting their products from patent infringers (James Dyson has written a book detailing the long years of struggle that went in to his eventual success).

Filing an application that may ultimately be granted in the US

If Gavin, our example TTMC founder, wants to explore the possibility of filing a patent for his unusual desk accessory, it is possible for him to start off the application process in the UK. There are international agreements in place between countries which ensure that a patent application filed anywhere in the world gives you patent pending status for 12 months. This presents a way of saving money by filing the initial patent application in your home country, even if your patent is unlikely to be ultimately granted there. Likewise, you do not need to go to the initial expense of engaging a patent attorney in another country.

Subsequently, you progress (or 'prosecute', to use the legal term) your application in the country in which you expect to secure your patent. Alternatively, one of your options would be to go on to file a Patent Co-operation Treaty application to protect your position internationally for a further 18 months before you need to decide on the countries in which to progress your patent.

Once you get to the stage of selecting countries, there will be translation costs to factor into your calculations as well as ongoing renewal fees. So, unless you are going to generate sufficient revenue from the patented product to justify such fees, you will be spending a lot of money without getting the gains to justify the cost of obtaining a patent monopoly.

When deciding whether to progress your patenting, be as rigorous as you would be with a new business idea. Is there really a gap in the market for it? Don't be so attached to the idea that you lose your objectivity in assessing its potential. You want to avoid filing a patent application for what are extremely weak patents.

Trade secrecy as alternative to patenting

Sometimes, keeping an otherwise patentable invention a trade secret may be a better option than patenting. Avoiding patent costs can be a cost-effective option if you are still able to exploit its value, for example by licensing the invention to others under an appropriate agreement imposing strict confidentiality obligations.

If you decide not to patent your invention, be aware that trade secrets do not stop others from inventing the same process or product independently. If a third party independently came up with the same invention and applied to patent 'your invention', you would have no rights to object to their being granted a patent. But you would still be able to use your invention within your own business without infringing on their patent, provided you had proof of your earlier invention. Be sure to maintain good records so you can show proof of the date you invented it, and your use of it.

In Gavin's case, as his innovation is a desk accessory which has a particular functionality that competitors could figure out by examining the product, it is unlikely that keeping the innovation a trade secret is an option for him.

With some patentable inventions, it is feasible to protect the underlying information by maintaining secrecy and imposing contractual obligations on those who have access to it. In such an instance, it's critically important that your trade secret information remains confidential. Using appropriate confidentiality obligations is key, as is having good internal procedures for looking after the information and imposing similar obligations on third parties to care for the information.

If anyone breached your confidentiality, and you could prove it, you would potentially have recourse to legal action. However, suing others is little comfort if they have no assets, and yet your information will have lost its confidential status and its value. So don't draw too much comfort from the fact that someone is prepared to sign your confidentiality undertaking.

More importantly, be careful to whom you reveal your information. Third parties could freely use the information if it fell into the public domain. You cannot prevent a third party using your information unless they were implicated in the unauthorised disclosure of the information.

Coca-Cola

Coca-Cola kept its recipe secret rather than filing a patent for it. Reportedly, it restricted access to its recipe to just three key employees worldwide at any one time. This way, the Coca-Cola recipe was kept secret for well over 100 years. With a patent, it would only have had, at most, 20 years' monopoly. On expiry of that monopoly the recipe would have been available for anyone to use. So, by opting for trade secrecy over patenting, Coca-Cola has been able to have exclusivity for a considerable period of time.

Patents are the strongest forms of monopoly, but patents and confidentiality aside, the law effectively protects your ideas from being copied through the name you use, your visual get-up, and through copyright law.

Conclusion

An in-depth conversation with a brand lawyer is a good way to understand what intellectual property you may have, and how to safeguard it from being copied by competitors. It's an excellent opportunity to work out what your strategy will be when it comes to securing your IP as the business moves forward. Depending on how important it is to your company to secure its IP assets as the business grows and develops, you may want to put in place systems and procedures and use contract templates within the business to ensure that copyright, trade mark and confidentiality considerations are always addressed at the appropriate time and in the appropriate way.

Chapter 8: Key take-home messages

■ Aim to secure as many different IP rights as is possible for each element of your brand or product.

■ Think carefully before making your best ideas public. Could it give your competitors an unfair advantage?

■ Allow sufficient lead time to bring your ideas to fruition before revealing them.

■ Don't be so attached to an idea that you lose your objectivity in assessing its potential.

■ If your idea is patentable, file the patent application before discussing your idea with investors.

■ You might have to spend valuable time and resources on protecting your patented product – keeping it a trade secret may be a better and more cost-effective option.

Chapter 9

Ways to build your brand on social media without risking your reputation

'A brand is no longer what we tell the consumer it is – it is what consumers tell each other it is' Scott Cook, co-founder of Intuit

Internet technologies have made it possible for ordinary people to post content online without the help of web designers skilled in HTML. 'Web 2.0' refers to these blogging technologies and the changes they spawned. These innovations are behind the birth of social media and explain why we are now able to interact and communicate with one another online so easily.

We saw the impact of social media and the Internet most keenly in 2011 with political uprisings in the Middle East spurred on by the sharing of information through services such as Twitter.

Social media has caught on far more rapidly than the time it took for radio, television or even the Internet itself to achieve such widespread use. This has resulted in phenomenal changes in the way we all communicate with one another. It has also radically transformed the way brands engage with customers.

Nowadays, nearly every major brand and celebrity personality – as well as many a savvy small business – has a presence in the world of social media. That presence may be a page (or multiple pages) on Facebook, a Twitter feed, a blog or an interactive section of the corporate or personal web page.

However, though it is relatively easy to gain a social media presence, it is decidedly more difficult to develop a cohesive strategy for using social media to promote your business.

How to engage online

Social media is still in its infancy, relatively speaking, and people are working out what their norms of behaviour should be on the different platforms, the main ones being Twitter, LinkedIn, YouTube, Google+ and Facebook. New social media sites are being set up all the time and it's increasingly challenging for organisations to keep up and know which ones to engage with and which to ignore.

Social media therefore throws up many new questions for businesses and business owners about how to engage online and protect their brand.

Pre-social media, it was easier for marketing and advertising agencies to influence and shape consumers' impressions of the brands they were helping to promote, but social media has altered the ways in which businesses promote themselves. As consumers discuss products and services they've experienced online, they become an important new dimension for businesses to address. Delivering excellent customer service is key to success in the new online environment.

Monitoring

So many people are engaging in discussions on the web and commenting on blogs, forums and social media sites, sometimes anonymously, and this is one reason why companies are finding it necessary to keep up with these trends and monitor the digital space.

Whether a company is a web-based business or a bricks and mortar one, conversations about it will take place online. So it makes sense to listen to, and even to take part in, these conversations because management of business reputation is a key component of successful brand building. (In this context, I am using the word 'brand' to mean a tool for growing the business profitably.)

For many companies, a presence on social media sites is indispensable for building brand awareness, interacting with consumers, and – if done right – increasing consumer trust. Some companies have even come up with innovative ideas for making money out of their presence on platforms such as Facebook.

Despite the rapid changes, we are still at an early stage in this revolution. What is undoubtedly true is that the increasing influence and reach of digital word of mouth makes it even more important to deliver excellent customer service, and to be aware of what is being said about your brand online. This matters both for promoting the brand and for protecting it.

Keep tabs on your online reputation

A happy customer may pass on their feelings to a few of their friends, but a disgruntled customer will pass on their concerns even more widely. Social networking means the 'disgruntled customer' effect quickly accelerates and an unfavourable write-up of your company or product can be quickly exposed to a potential audience of thousands, if not millions of Internet users.

While Google is undoubtedly the quickest way to gauge your online reputation, it's hardly the entire picture. Finding out what's being said about yourself or your company online needs to take account of all blogs, microblogs (such as Twitter), social networking, video sharing websites, news feeds, forums, message boards and whatever other new buzz tool Web 2.0 throws up this week.

There are a variety of free tools online, such as Google Alerts, that will allow you to search through sites or monitor them in real time, but keeping tabs on everything can be complicated, confusing and time-consuming. As a result, an increasing number of companies and individuals are using external reputation monitoring services to keep track of their online reputation. These services will monitor keywords, such as names of key

Questions, and more questions continually arise on social media

- Is it copyright infringement to pin a photo on Pinterest?

- Did Phonedog own the account of an employee simply because the Twitter handle was in its name @Phonedog_Noah?

- How does the Meltwater case affect the way I can link to articles?

- Can a court order be served on Twitter?

- Am I liable if someone defames someone else in a comment on my blog?

- How can I send a takedown notice if I don't know who was behind an anonymous post?

- Can my employer retain rights over my LinkedIn?

staff, or topics that the business is interested in. It's also relevant to monitor competitors too.

The best defence is a good offence, and if you're already out there on the Internet engaging with your customers via blogs and social networking, you're in a good position to promote your reputation by being honest, transparent, and positive.

And that's good business.

Online comments

One aspect of comments that make them a matter of serious concern is that they can be instantly and indefinitely accessible to millions of people around the world.

If a consumer is dissatisfied with a product or service, Web 2.0 makes it possible for them to broadcast their disappointment, not just to their immediate circle of friends, but worldwide. This takes on more sinister significance as what may have previously been a grumble down the pub heard by a handful of people is captured, and remains there for everyone to see, possibly for years.

Alisher Usmanov: A cause célèbre

When Alisher Usmanov, the Ukrainian billionaire and major shareholder of the Arsenal Football Club, hired Shillings, a firm of libel law specialists, to try to take down the blog belonging to Craig Murray (an ex-ambassador from the United Kingdom to the Ukraine who had written about Usmanov's alleged criminal activities during his rise to power), Usmanov came up against the unwieldiness of the Internet.

Far from managing to remove Murray's blog posts, press interest was increased when Fasthosts, which was hosting Murray's website, pulled the plug on all the websites for which Murray's site administrator was responsible in the face of the administrator's refusal to take down Murray's site. It was unfortunate that the administrator's sites included the website of Boris Johnson and the London Bach Society. The incident also became a cause célèbre in the blogging world when many prominent bloggers began commenting on the case, and others posted Murray's blog on US sites, out of the jurisdiction of the legal action.

Unless you actually own the site on which negative content appears, getting content removed on the web is difficult, if not impossible. You may succeed in getting one site to take down content, only to see that content resurface elsewhere, or the comment remains cached in a search engine or appears on other websites or blogs.

The important point is that whether there is any validity to online smears is immaterial. Once a smear is on the Internet it's in the public sphere, where it stays. It needs to be handled with care.

As people react more and more to names and reputations, to rumours and word-of-mouth activity taking place online, management of digital word of mouth is more necessary than ever. Being able to respond quickly and appropriately to whatever is discovered is one of the fundamental pillars of online reputation management.

Defamation and other laws

One common situation where a brand may need to resort to litigation is where there is damage to its reputation, for example, if someone defames the brand.

Case study: Applause Store

In the *Applause Store Productions* (2008) case, a man was held liable for comments made on Facebook.

The case is interesting because of the way the court responded. The case involved Mathew Firsht, owner of Applause Store Productions, a well-known company which provides audiences for television shows. Mathew did not have a Facebook account. In June 2007 a fake profile was placed on Facebook in an account under Mr Firsht's name. It featured extensive personal information, including his sexual orientation, political views, religious beliefs and a picture of himself – which was actually a copy of his twin brother's profile picture.

The profile also included a link to a Facebook Group called 'Has Mathew Firsht lied to you?' There was no dispute about whether the material was defamatory, but only over who had published it.

The defendant, a Mr Raphael who was a friend of Mr Firsht and knew him professionally, had his identity revealed after Firsht's lawyers sent a takedown notice to Facebook and obtained a Norwich Pharmacal order. This is the name of the court order that is necessary to require disclosure of personal information as to the identity of a person. The order required Facebook to disclose not only the registration data, but also details of the IP addresses and email addresses used when creating the profile.

The profile had in fact been created by someone at Mr Raphael's IP address. The same IP address was also used during this time to log in to two other Facebook accounts: Mr Raphael's account and Mr Raphael's girlfriend's account. The fake account had only been signed into from two different computers at the IP address: Mr Raphael's computer and his girlfriend's laptop. These facts were not refuted by Mr Raphael.

The case gets even stranger. Mr Raphael's defence was that he did not create the profile. The evening the profile was created, he and his girlfriend had met a group of strangers at a bar, who returned home with them and spent the night there. He said that one of them must have created the profile from his computer. He could not give an explanation of how someone else had been logging into the account from his IP address on the subsequent times the account had been accessed ... which would have been after the profile-creating stranger had left his home. Instead he chose to rely on alibi evidence that he had not been at home on the other occasions when the Facebook profile had been accessed.

The judge couldn't quite believe this story. He decided that Mr Raphael had been the one to put up the false profile and the defamatory group. Although the profile was not visible for a long time – only 16 days – the judge ruled that due to the popularity and nature of Facebook, which targeted the material towards people who knew Mr Firsht personally, the materials were particularly damaging.

The judge also ruled that the allegations of dishonesty were serious enough to harm Mr Firsht's business and awarded £15,000 to Mr Firsht personally, £5,000 to his business and an extra £2,000 for breach of his privacy. In this case, Mr Raphael learned to his chagrin that comments made online can be costly and that lawyers can often get around the anonymity problem easily.

Beware how you approach online brand protection

Because trying to protect your reputation online can backfire badly, you need to think carefully about how to respond to situations you come across, and consult a brand lawyer rather than taking action yourself. You would not expect legal action that you take for damage to your reputation to end up harming you more. However, online this is precisely what can happen due to the way the Internet alters the legal approach you might otherwise adopt.

To unmask anonymous posters, sending threatening letters and initiating court proceedings are an option. Indeed, such steps may be used to bully Internet service providers and forums into removing material, even the kind that's only arguably defamatory. This is because entities lose their immunity from legal action for content that they host once they receive notice of the existence of objectionable content. Therefore, some administrators do cave in and simply remove offending material.

However, take a look at the case of Barbra Streisand and Alisher Usmanov and you'll appreciate why 'Streisand Effect' is now a term for taking a heavy-handed legal approach to suppress information that ends up backfiring and, indeed, magnifying publicity for the information you were aiming to have removed.

The 'Streisand Effect'

Barbra Streisand had discovered that a certain Internet site was featuring a photo of her house. She took legal action to have the photograph taken down on the grounds that it was an invasion of her privacy to have it online. She lost the case because the photographer successfully argued that he was studying the effects of coastal erosion – her house just happened to be on the edge of a coastal cliff. The outcome was far worse than she could have anticipated. The legal action attracted a lot of attention and there was a tenfold increase in the amount of traffic to the website holding the picture. The image is now prominently displayed on Wikipedia.

Anonymity Online

A significant proportion of the material posted online is anonymous because people often use pseudonyms or no name at all. As mentioned above, the recourse that is available when infringing or defamatory material is posted anonymously is to apply to a court for a Norwich Pharmacal order to obtain the IP address of the poster. That is, if you intend to take legal action on the infringing or defamatory comment.

IP addresses are associated with Internet connections, but they are not necessarily permanent. Someone may have one IP address one day and a different one the next. To conclusively identify the owner of an Internet connection, you must obtain personal information from an Internet service provider. That is why in *Applause* the information as to the identity of the creator of the account could not be freely offered by Facebook, but had to be mandated by the court to divulge the information.

For material posted on your own site, you will have the commenter's IP address. If the material was posted from within a large company, you might be able to use this to trace it to that company, but not to a specific person within it. If the anonymous content is not on your site, you will need a court order to find out the IP address behind it. Wireless networks can make things more difficult. If they are secure, then there's no real difference between wireless and non-wireless in being able to identify the user, but if they are left unsecured, then someone could have simply been passing by and used it.

International v. local jurisdiction

One of problems with online content is the international nature of the Internet compared to the local jurisdiction of the courts. This means that if someone is featuring content that's damaging about you and they move it to a server in another country, there is little a UK court can do to help you have the damaging content removed.

Where the site is owned by someone based in the UK, it's possible to take action against the owner of the website for publishing the material. However, unless they are the author of the material, website owners are protected by the EU e-commerce regulations, which grant immunity to owners who are merely responsible or hosting the material. This is the reason why some site administrators may voluntarily remove content if they are notified. They do not want to risk their site losing its immunity and becoming personally responsible. However, they will often need notification from solicitors, detailing in what way the content they are hosting infringes on others' rights.

Some hosts may be willing to remove offending material in response to an amicable request, supported by clear rationale. However, if a site is outside the jurisdiction, for example located in the US, the rules are somewhat different, and the position needs to be carefully assessed so as to avoid unwittingly attracting attention to damaging content.

Keeping track

In order to keep track of the effect of your marketing projects or to find out about damaging comments, you can use the tools that have been developed to monitor sentiment and online discussion.

Once you've set up a range of RSS feeds to capture content, you will have access to material that could be used to identify opportunities to sell your products and services as well as to pick up on bad press or customer dissatisfaction early on.

The free tools available are probably a good starting point for SMEs looking to monitor their reputation. Even for large organisations, they have a place at the departmental level to keep track of online conversations that are more interesting to that particular department than to the organisation as a whole. The organisation would use a paid monitoring service to keep track of issues of significance to the board. Free tools include Google Alerts which notify you whenever new mentions of your chosen keywords are found, and these alerts can be aggregated using RSS feeds into a single stream on Google Reader. A simple search through Google will turn up a wealth of information on Google Alerts, RSS feeds and Google Reader.

Catching bad press early is important, because it allows you to respond in good time before it has time to circulate or escalate. There are services that will collect information from password protected social media sites too. Some will sift through irrelevant hits and save you time, but for smaller brands, who are not mentioned much, it may not be necessary to have a filtering service or to use more sophisticated tools.

Personal branding v. business branding

In the social media environment, a new issue to address – which particularly affects small business owners – is how to handle your business and personal identity on the Internet, given that it is increasingly necessary to engage personally online. It is difficult to hide behind a corporate identity and simply promote the business's brand.

The blog has become the basic pillar on which individuals and corporates build their brands in the arena of social media. It has sparked off a 'personal branding' revolution that social media engagement continues to fuel.

On microblogging sites such as Twitter or on other social media platforms, it may be wise to have the owner of the business or its CEO (if the business is a large one) at the heart of the business's tweets. A more colourful Twitter presence will result in greater engagement with the business than a bland, anonymous corporate account.

When Tom Peters wrote *The Brand You 50* (Knopf) in 1999, branding was a strategic issue in many sectors of business. His book saw the start of what has become the personal branding industry. Whether you are an employee or a business owner, the prevailing wisdom is that you will be more marketable and successful if you develop yourself as a brand.

The disruptive effect of social media has changed the established order of many industries, so that many unprecedented questions about branding are arising for business owners, including how they should balance the business' brand with the development of a higher profile for themselves.

A pressing question for companies is how to balance the competing interests of their business's brand with those of individuals representing it on social media, when networking online. What are the considerations if employees and founders of the business are promoting their own personal brands on social media? Does it detract from the business? What are the issues to guard against?

If the business owner's personality dominated the business so that their following on social media platforms was far greater than that of the business, would prospective purchasers of the business feel that the business could not exist without the owner? What should Gavin, our fictitious business owner, do to make sure he has a business to sell that could be developed and grown? The need to think about how you brand yourself as a person on social media as against how you brand your business, and coming up with a naming strategy, is an issue that business owners invariably find challenging.

Building the brand online – small business owners

The ideal is to align the brand building that you or your staff does with the goals and values of the business.

At our example business, TTMC, the benefit of Gavin's own personal brand will generally transfer to the business once the business becomes better known. In the early days, what matters is to get the business off the ground, and to use whatever it takes to do this, namely whether to use the business owner's own personality or that of other employees, for example Casper.

Later, once the business is successful, it should gain followers in its own right.

For instance, Apple has its own devoted fans that are quite separate from those who were devoted followers of the late Steve Jobs.

The HubSpot business, like Apple, also has a large following in its own right.

HubSpot

If you compare its ratio of followers to the follower ratios of its founders, Dharmesh Shah and Brian Halligan, it's clear that Hubspot is more popular than either of the founders. The business's success exceeds that of the founders, despite the fact that both of them have a high profile and promote their own personal brands.

One of these founders has his own separate business, OnStartups.com, so this is another reason why it makes sense for Gavin, our fictitious business owner, to have a separate individual profile on social media platforms and another one for any ventures in which he may engage in future. Many entrepreneurs are likely to be associated with more than one business.

Creating a business that you are likely to be selling or retiring from within a given number of years doesn't mean you have to try to minimise your own personality. Rather, it requires the opposite, while at the same time constructing a business that can run without you – in the way that it could function without your hands-on presence, should you be absent for a few months. That's a completely separate issue from whether you promote your personal brand or not. Richard Branson has many businesses, all of which undoubtedly survive without him even though he is a dominant character in the Virgin brand.

Twitter

Possibly the single most important social media platform for a brand is Twitter. As social media is still in its infancy there is no accepted norm for how to behave on channels such as this. Those who use Twitter as a channel to engage and interact with other users – 'responders' – talk disparagingly of 'broadcasters' who use it primarily as a microblogging platform. Broadcasters, on the other hand, consider Twitter to be more of a news channel than a social networking platform.

Generally speaking, responders are considered to be those who have streams filled with @ commands and who would commonly follow lots of people. Broadcasters tend not to follow many people, and won't necessarily feel the need to respond to @ notes or direct messages.

Pete Cashmore, of Mashable fame, has more than 20,000 followers and follows less than 5% of those. His Twitter stream shows little sign of engagement, so he might be described as falling into the broadcasting camp. However, as the founder of Mashable, he can't be dismissed as someone ignorant of proper Twitter use, which is how the responders tend to think of the broadcasters.

But there are no hard and fast rules about the best approach to adopt on Twitter. How you behave may depend, in part, on which of these two camps you lean towards. If you believe Twitter is all about engagement and is a great way to build relationships, you'll also be trying to promote other people. You're likely to 'retweet' people you know – that is, share their messages with your followers – partly because they have an interesting update, but also to help them to get noticed. You'll believe that joining conversations and answering questions is the best way to create relationships. On the other hand, if you fall into the other camp, you'll tend to use it as a place to post links to your blog posts and press releases and not engage in a lot of conversations.

Names and Avatars

Throughout this book, we've looked at the importance of the name you choose for your business. But what about your own personal name? Is there anything you can do to make yourself stand out more on social media if you don't have a memorable and unique name?

Our fictitious business owner, Gavin Brown, may need to take action if he is to attract the right kind of attention online. The solution is for Gavin to adopt the ideas of David Meerman Scott in his book *The New Rules of Marketing and PR* (John Wiley, 2011). David explains the importance of having a stand-out brand. Had he just used his name David Scott, it would have been difficult for people to find him online when they searched for him. Instead, he opted to add his unusual middle name so that he would have a greater chance of being unique online.

So Gavin at TTMC might make use of his middle name so as to have a more memorable name. He should check whether he can register the .com and co.uk versions of the name and, if so, register them. At the same time, he might check that he can secure the same name on as many of the main social media platforms as possible. These would include Google+, Facebook, Twitter, YouTube, LinkedIn.

Whether you are considering your own profile or that of the business, the aim is to try to feature in the first ten results in Google or other search engines, so that when others search for your personal or business name they will easily find you. Building your Google profile is invaluable because the first place that people look for more information about you is on the web. If you have a solid online presence, and own the top ten links for both your own name and your company name, it will help to attract enquiries about you and is also an important way to protect your online reputation. Adopt a similar approach with your business name. If you are still undecided on the name, it's worth checking the availability of names for online profiles for your business, as well as making the other checks outlined in Chapter 12 that are necessary when choosing a new name and registering it as a trade mark.

Keywords v. names

We looked at keywords in Chapter 4, and these need careful thought when setting up an online brand and assessing how searchers will find the answers to problems they face. Keywords are just as relevant for social media. But when it comes to choosing your avatar (that is the graphical representation of yourself, such as your photo and name), it's not a good idea to use a keyword-rich name, for the same reasons a descriptive name is not a good choice for a brand name.

Google gives prominence to the keyword, when determining whose website and information to deliver in response to surfers' searches for products or services of the type you sell. However, on social media, keywords are not the primary way in which people will notice you. On social media, people are engaging with others and so are more likely to look for and remember people they know by name. So, it would make less sense for Gavin to tweet as (for example) '@ManageTime', than under his real name.

If your own name is unavailable on a platform, you may be able to add a description to your name so that people looking for you will still find you. Alternatively, you might add an initial instead of a middle name. Ideally, try to find a uniform name that you can use across all platforms, and which you can register as your .com and .co.uk personal domain. For the same reason, use the same avatar (that is, photograph) across all platforms so that people who know you on one platform can readily identify you on another.

But what do you do if you find that your desired username is already registered or is being misused online? Let's deal with that next.

Recovering usernames on social media

Having a registered trade mark will generally give you stronger remedies for recovering a username on most social media sites if someone else has registered 'your' name. It depends on why that individual has registered the same name on a social media site, and how the name is being used. The rules for recovery of a name on social media sites vary, and often may require you to establish trade mark infringement in order to recover a name.

When it comes to your trade marked name, Facebook, YouTube and Twitter all have a system in place for complaining about infringing usernames. In most situations, using the social media and social networking sites' own reporting policies will be an appropriate option initially rather than resorting to litigation. Facebook can transfer the username, but the account handler can't do it themselves.

Twitter username policy

Twitter allows parody impersonations – that's where the intention is to poke fun, mock, or comment on someone – if they are clearly parody, commentary or fan accounts. However, the social media site's policy is not set in stone. They have to deal with situations as they emerge and they may act on feedback to adapt that approach for future use. If somebody has registered your name, and is using it for a different purpose that does not trade on your goodwill or pretend to be you, it would not be feasible to claim the name from the account holder. So, for example, if my brand name were Zumba and someone else had got to Twitter first and registered Zumba, and was using it as their personal account handle, but in no way pretending to be Zumba or to have any connection with the dance, it's unlikely Twitter would confiscate the name from them.

Where there is a trade mark use issue at play, Twitter's response is likely to be quite different. For example, in a case involving Girl Geeks in 2011, Twitter transferred the account @girlgeeks to a person who had registered a logo mark incorporating the words 'Girl Geeks' in a stylised font with the image of a girl sitting on the 'girl' part of the name. In trade mark law, a logo mark does not give exclusive rights over the word included in the registration. What's more, the original account holder had used their Twitter account for two years.

Twitter's trade mark policy stipulated that some uses of the service may be considered trade mark infringement, allowing a trade mark owner to recover the username. Where there is a clear intent to mislead others through the unauthorised use of a trade mark, Twitter will suspend the account and notify the account holder. If this is not intentional, the infringer has an opportunity to clear up any potential confusion to avoid losing the account.

In this instance Twitter seemingly took the side of the trade mark owner and considered there to be a clear intent to mislead others, as according to the blog piece the original owner was simply given notice that her account was to be changed from #girlgeeks to #girl_geeks_ (that is, adding an underscore before and after geeks). The trade mark owner whose lawyers had initiated the complaint, was herself surprised with Twitter's actions as she had hoped to mediate the issue with the original owner and had not expected that Twitter would simply hand over the account to her.

This is indicative of Twitter's general approach of giving preference to registered trade mark owners, and I've also known Facebook to adopt a similar approach too. The account is transferred and the person whose account has been transferred then needs to complain to Facebook if they want to. The social media sites want to take a quick view and avoid the need to mediate lengthy disputes between the parties. Giving preference to a registered trade mark owner often works for them.

Generally speaking social media sites' policies enable you to recover usernames, if the content on a page would confuse users into believing that you, the trade mark owner, created or sponsored the page or its content. There has been some litigation on this that illustrates the points that can arise.

> In *Oneok v. Twitter, Inc*, a third party registered the Oneok username and sent out tweets using both the Oneok trade mark and logo. Oneok sued primarily on the basis that the user intended to deceive others. Twitter took down the account the next day and the case was dismissed.

> In *Anthony LaRussa v. Twitter, Inc*, a third party registered twitter.com/TonyLaRussa and impersonated Tony LaRussa, a well-known baseball player. Tony LaRussa filed a lawsuit for infringement, dilution, cybersquatting and misappropriation of name and likeness. The case was settled, but Twitter now has policies that address impersonation, though they no longer have Verified Accounts available to the public.

Conclusion

Social media is a great way to build the brand online. Engaging on social media platforms also helps you protect your business in the event that it receives negative press. This makes it even more important to have a brand name that helps you to stand out both as a business and personally as an entrepreneur, and having a memorable name is the way to achieve this. Producing good content is also fundamental to online success, as is monitoring online conversations.

Chapter 9: Key take-home messages

■ Having a prominent presence on social media sites helps you to interact with your customers and – if done right – increase their trust.

■ Develop a strategy for balancing the competing interests of your brand with those of individuals representing it on social media.

■ Take advantage of the tools that monitor online discussion so you can keep track of your online reputation, or consider using an external reputation monitoring service.

■ Catching bad press early allows you to respond in good time before it has time to circulate or escalate.

■ Consult a brand lawyer rather than taking action yourself – or it could backfire badly.

Chapter 10

Navigating the minefield of changing laws when doing business online

'The best way to get a bad law repealed is to enforce it' Abraham Lincoln

Many questions crop up for brands online. These include aspects of domain names, use of cookies and other data protection laws, and the rules about trade mark use, including the sale of counterfeit goods.

The Internet tends to give rise to new business models such as online search advertising services and online auction marketplaces like eBay. This has presented many questions for the courts and law-making bodies in the EU.

These rapid technological changes inevitably challenge the law as it finds its existing answers inadequate to deal with the constant stream of new problems that need to be resolved. People inevitably turn to the courts for help to address the new issues they face, but the cases move through the system very slowly.

Google AdWords

One such line of cases has involved balancing the interests of new services such as Google Adwords with the competing interests of brand owners whose trade marks are being used online in novel ways by competitors.

One series of cases has revolved around the rules relating to how others use trade marks online, such as to advertise on Google Adwords or in online auction forums like eBay.

In this chapter we'll look at the broad principles of this issue while the blog for this book, on www.legallybranded.co.uk, will watch out for and report on new developments in this area.

What are Google AdWords?

Pay per click (PPC) advertising, also known as 'paid search' advertising, involves paying to appear on the first page of a search engine when someone searches for the term or phrase you've purchased.

Google Adwords is the most well-known example of this, and in this chapter I'll use it as a shorthand reference to denote the style of advertising it represents. There are many other search engines and social media sites, including Yahoo, Bing, and Facebook, that operate such advertising.

For any questions concerning advertising on these platforms, you will need to review that particular site's policy on keyword advertising as each site has its own trade mark policies, some of which might differ according to the geographic location of a trade mark holder.

Google AdWords basics

The way the advertising works is that if you paid for the term 'managing time, London', for instance, you'd be paying to have an advertisement for your site appear on the first page of Google when someone searched for that particular phrase. Pay per click literally means you only pay for your ad when someone clicks on it.

How pay per click works

In order to get their ads listed high in the 'paid search' results for Google's or other search engines' networks, advertisers bid on keywords. So, if the amount being paid per click for a keyword like 'computer equipment' were £3.06, then Google or other search engines would keep the entire amount if the click on the advertiser's ad came directly from the results displayed on its own pages.

But Google also sub-contracts ads to others who are part of the wider 'content network' (Google AdSense). These third party sites would also display the ad. For example, you will notice on Amazon, that there are some ads which relate to the topic you are looking at. So if you click on the advertiser's ad on Amazon, say, then Google would share the £3.06 with Amazon. Third party sites which host Google's ads are known as 'click farmers' in the industry; some of these will be legitimate businesses and others will belong to cybersquatters.

Click farming thrives, partly because of the 15–20% of Internet users who type a URL into a web browser rather than entering the keyword into a search engine. So, if instead of doing a Google search to see which sites come up for 'managingtime' I type in the URL www.managingtime.com' I arrive at a click farming site. The person using this search method will not necessarily know what site will appear, if any when searching in this way. A common way that trade mark infringers or cybersquatters, as they are also called, use this to their advantage is to register mistypings of a brand's URL, so that when it is entered into the browser, they benefit from this 'direct navigation' traffic (as opposed to indirect traffic through a search engine like Google). The mistyped address leads straight to the page at which the domain is 'parked' (i.e. the place the domain address arrives at), or to its website if there is one, as there sometimes will be. Then ads relevant to that brand will be displayed on the page in question. So, in the case of Microsoft, before it took the action mentioned in Chapter 16, various misspellings of its name were leading to cybersquatters' pages featuring ads for software and computer products.

What if your trade mark is used?

If you find that your brand name is registered by someone else as a domain name, and is being used in this way for click farming purposes, or is just being held without being used, it may be worth establishing whether you have any possibility of recovering the domain name from these third parties. Recovery might be possible if you satisfy the conditions of the registering authority of the domain name in question (more about this in Chapter 16).

But what if the trade mark is used in AdWords?

A relatively simple phrase like 'wedding DJ Manchester', which uses generic descriptive words, won't raise many red flags, even if someone claims it is 'their brand name' and you are trespassing by bidding on the term.

But what if another business uses the Google AdWords or other platforms to purchase keywords that are trade marked, whether they are heavyweight brands like Vuitton or lesser-known trade marks such as Portakabin? The effect of an advertiser bidding on a trade mark keyword means they may buy advertising space next to that brand and then see their competing advert pop up in the sponsored links section on Google or other platforms when an Internet user searches the trade mark keyword in Google.

By paying for advertising space for the search term 'Vuitton', a user could drive traffic to a website selling counterfeit handbags, or a legitimate business reselling second-hand Vuitton bags, or even promoting a site that delivers something entirely different to the merchandise that Vuitton sells.

All these possibilities essentially piggyback on the brand associated with the trade marked keyword Vuitton. Such practices force the legitimate owners of a trade mark into a bidding war over a keyword that is their own trade mark.

Trade mark use by competitors

Understandably, many trade mark owners are unhappy when they see others using their trade marks in this way, and litigation has ensued.

Being part of the European Union means that national courts who are asked to hear such cases will often conclude that there are policy decisions involved in the cases which require them to refer the issues to the Court of Justice of the European Union (CJEU). The case is then referred to the CJEU, and the upshot is that the dispute is only resolved by the English court once the CJEU has given judgment guiding the national court on how to approach the decision-making in this particular case.

So, once the question that the CJEU was asked to answer has been dealt with, the case is sent back to the national courts for a decision. The English court has the benefit of the CJEU's guidance in determining the particular dispute.

Such Internet-related issues in trade mark law are a fast-moving, rapidly changing area and there have been many decisions, such as *L'Oréal v. eBay, LVMH v. eBay* and numerous Google cases. But, here, my intention is to give you a general idea of the pivotal points on issues such as Google and eBay's liability as service providers, rather than to survey the litigation that has taken place in any depth.

These cases are difficult for the law. It's invariably faced with the question of whether existing laws are adequate to deal with new issues the Internet throws up. Do we need to develop new laws to address these matters, or are there existing principles within which these issues can be made to fit neatly? If new laws are needed, the legislative process will take a long time to introduce them.

When technology develops as fast as it does on the Internet, the danger is that, no sooner are certain issues dealt with, than new ones pop up that the new laws do not adequately address.

That is why companies like Google need to feel comfortable with pushing the boundaries of the law when they want to introduce new products or services that could potentially breach the law. Before we look at these, bear in mind that the words 'trade mark use' and 'trade mark infringement' have specific meanings (see Chapter 15).

Google's role

Google, being the owner of the system that facilitates many of the alleged infringements, has itself been the natural target of some of the litigation.

With respect to the Google AdWords service, the courts have decided that, by providing the service, Google cannot be said to be 'using' the trade mark of others on its goods and services within the meaning of trade mark law. As an 'information society service provider', a term used in EU law, Google enjoys exemption from liability under the law. It is merely providing the platform to enable one business to bid on a keyword that is the trade mark of another business. Google is granted immunity under the law, where its conduct is neutral.

Why information society services are exempt

Information society services (ISS) are the backbone of the Internet, providing referencing services such as Google or hosting or other facilities on the Internet, by way of forums or social media platforms like Twitter, Facebook, and LinkedIn. Those merely providing platforms such as online marketplaces like eBay are also classed as 'information society services'.

Information society services provide facilities that are often used for lawful purposes, but may also be used for unlawful purposes. EU laws were introduced at the beginning of the millennium to grant immunity to these services, where they are both neutral, and have been unaware of the acts of infringement and taken action when notified about the infringement.

In Google's case, the CJEU found Google was an ISS within the definition of EU law (a Directive). In terms of determining whether Google was exempt under the Directive, the court made a number of points before deciding that national courts were 'best placed to be aware of the actual terms on which the service ... is supplied'.

The fact that Google is paid for its AdWords service does not prevent it from having the benefit of the immunity that the law provides to information society services. However, if Google were to assist people in drafting their ads it could potentially lose the immunity granted by the EU Directive.

An important point highlighted in the Google judgment on the Directive is that a service provider 'cannot be held liable for the data which it has stored at the request of an advertiser ...' unless it is notified that it is holding unlawful data. For example, if the advertiser is selling counterfeit goods using a Google Adwords campaign, then Google must act quickly to remove or disable access to the account if it is to avoid losing its immunity.

So the exemption implies a positive obligation on the service provider to 'take down' infringing content. If it failed to do so, then it would forgo the exemption provided under the Directive.

In light of the courts' involvement, Google became more proactive and updated its policies to allow a complaints procedure for both keyword bidding and trade marks in ad text within the EU.

But this is a double-edged sword for trade mark owners. A result of the CJEU ruling is that Google now makes it possible for the entire EU market to bid on trade mark keywords, but with the proviso that they will also deal with keyword complaints. The new policy moves most of the EU countries from a position where trade mark keywords were restricted from bids, to allowing trade mark keywords to be bid upon.

Liability of advertisers bidding on keywords

Another aspect of the issues is this: if Google is not liable for trade mark infringement, then what about the advertisers themselves? By advertisers, I mean the businesses that use the AdWords service to bid on other people's trade marks as keywords.

The law is clear: bidding on keywords is 'trade mark use' by advertisers and that falls within the scope of trade mark law. Although advertisers are 'using' other brand owners' trade marks when they bid on them as keywords (as they are thereby making their adverts appear), the decisions have established that this use is not enough in itself to create an infringement.

The CJEU developed more appropriate principles for analysing AdWords trade mark disputes and updated the definition of the old trade mark term 'use' for the online world, creating a test to be applied by national courts to determine whether or not there is infringement.

For the use to be an infringement, there also has to be either an adverse effect on the function of a trade mark or a likelihood of confusion for consumers. A function of trade marks is to indicate the origin of goods and services. In other words, they enable customers to link the brand name or other 'sign' with the goods and services provided by the business. So the trade mark 'Vuitton' links to goods and services provided by the Louis Vuitton company.

The CJEU has also accepted that there are other functions worthy of being protected for a trade mark, namely 'guaranteeing the quality of the goods or services' in question, and those of communication, investment, advertising, and so on.

However, the CJEU was not convinced that these other functions were adversely affected simply by allowing trade marks to be used as keywords in sponsored link advertising. Focusing on the advertising function, the CJEU conceded that trade mark owners were being drawn into a bidding war with others over their own trade marks as keywords, resulting in them having to pay a 'higher price per click'.

The CJEU was nevertheless satisfied that trade mark owners' exposure was sufficient in the organic search results to reverse any adverse effect on advertising – 'the visibility to Internet users of the goods or services of the proprietor of the trade mark is guaranteed'.

To decide whether there was any adverse effect on the function or origin of a trade mark, the CJEU devised a specific test whereby one should look at the situation from the point of view of a 'normally informed and reasonably attentive Internet user'. The question is whether such a person would be able to tell whether the ad originated from the trade mark owner or from a third party.

In other words, if the person did a Google search on the keyword 'Vuitton', would he or she find it difficult to identify whether the ad originated from the Vuitton trade mark proprietor or the advertiser?

The CJEU thought that there would be trade mark infringement if the ad either suggested an economic link between the advertiser of the mark and the trade mark owner, or was vague as to the origin of the goods so that a 'normally informed and reasonably attentive' Internet user would have difficulty in identifying where the goods came from. This would be infringement as there would be an adverse effect on the function of the mark.

In conclusion, if you bid on a keyword and there is no suggestion of an economic link, trade mark infringement is less likely to take place.

Interflora v. Marks and Spencer

A case involving Interflora gave rise to the question of the liability of the advertiser. The case concerned a dispute over Marks and Spencer bidding in AdWords on the trade mark 'Interflora' to advertise its own flower delivery services.

Here, the High Court originally referred the question to the CJEU to clarify the law in this area. As this occurred before the Google judgment was delivered, the CJEU asked the High Court judge whether he wished to revise some of the ten questions put forward for the CJEU to consider in the case. After hearing observations from both sides, the judge decided to withdraw some of the questions, amended one, but kept four outstanding.

The CJEU reached its decision in September 2011, reiterating that use of a trade mark as a keyword to trigger a sponsored link is 'use' in the course of trade in relation to the advertiser's goods or services, even where the trade mark does not appear in the text of the advertisement.

Such use may only be prevented by the trade mark owner if it's likely to have an adverse effect on one of the functions of a trade mark. Essentially, the main function of a trade mark is to indicate the origin of goods and services. Within limits the law allows competitors to compare themselves to another brand, provided they win the consumer over to their product or service without damaging the reputation of the trade mark owner and they don't pretend that their product emanates from the trade mark owner.

So, for example, if I have a new type of fizzy drink to sell and want to use a brand with a reputation as a keyword to trigger my ads selling my own fizzy drinks, then I might bid on the Coca-Cola name as a keyword.

Doing so, to capture the attention of consumers who are interested in fizzy drinks, in the hope that they will buy mine instead of buying

Coca-Cola's is regarded as fair competition, provided it does nothing to damage the reputation of Coca-Cola or mislead consumers into thinking they are buying Coca-Cola when they are in fact buying my drink.

As Interflora's business model is such that flowers are sold under its brand by third party retailers, the question that the UK court now needs to decide is whether Marks and Spencer's advertising enabled the reasonably well-informed and observant Internet user to understand that Marks and Spencer was independent from Interflora, and was promoting its own flowers service. If it was, then its AdWords would not have infringed on the trade mark rights of Interflora.

What about 'natural (that is, not paid for) Google results'?

All of the cases so far relate to the use of trade marks in the context of AdWords or the sponsored links section in Google. But what of the natural results section of the service? Advertisers or competitors may develop expensive SEO campaigns on the basis of trade mark keywords to find themselves at the highest position in the natural results. What if, in order to save on AdWords, they targeted a competitor's trade mark name so they could be positioned in the search results next to its name whenever searchers searched for them? This could divert traffic away from the competitor's. Is it acceptable?

An argument raised by the Court of Appeal in the case of *Reed Executive plc v. Reed Business Information Ltd* [2004] was that the use of metatags was invisible to members of the public and thus use of trade marks in metatags may well not count as 'trade mark use' in the course of trade. While metatags and AdWords are different situations, both involve essentially invisible processes in terms of their public-facing aspects. In general, some people think that using keywords in metatags would amount to use as a trade mark while others think it wouldn't and there are different decisions from the national courts within the EU.

Interestingly, the European Court of Justice has refused on a number of occasions to evaluate whether use of a trade mark as a metatag to appear in the natural results constitutes 'trade mark use'. On every occasion that the question was posed to the Court it replied that there was no need to address this question because the facts of the case did not involve the use of keywords in metatags or the like.

The Court is essentially deferring the question to another time, possibly waiting to see the effects of the AdWords decisions first before carving out further policies. But it may be more than that. The Attorney General (whose role is to advise the CJEU) was careful to point out that allowing the scope of trade mark law into the natural search results would change the Internet as we know it.

eBay decisions

Another line of cases that has occupied the courts involve eBay.

These generally involve counterfeit goods and the extent of eBay's obligations as an information society service provider to monitor its site for counterfeit goods.

The issues before the court essentially turn on who should bear the burden of removing infringing material online? Is it the brand owner or is it the service provider?

How far must eBay and other service providers go to ensure they are not falling foul of trade mark law? Are they expected to become the policing agent of the brand owner? If they are expected to also have a policy of removing infringing content and repeat offenders, what does this policy look like?

L'Oréal case

The CJEU ruled in the *eBay v. L'Oréal* case that an Internet marketplace like eBay is not 'using' a trade mark just by allowing customers to display goods on its website. So if those goods were counterfeits or otherwise unlawfully imported into the EU, eBay would not be infringing the trade mark rights of the brand owners whose trade mark rights were infringed by the goods.

However, if eBay or other operators play an active role – or are aware of facts or circumstances that point to online offers for sale being unlawful and do not act promptly to remove them – they could lose their immunity, and so become liable to the brand owners for trade mark infringement. So, helping users, such as by providing services to optimise or promote their online offers for sale is best avoided by the ISS.

All in all, the CJEU's decision makes it likely that eBay will avoid playing an active role by reducing the services which could trigger such liability. It will need to tread a fine line between taking care not to attract liability by limiting the services that could expose it to litigation, while avoiding being wilfully blind to infringement when providing services which its legitimate, non-counterfeit users would expect to have.

Conclusion

It's clear that the questions surrounding the use of competitors' trade marks as keywords in advertising and as metatags have attracted much litigation. The overall picture is complicated, and there are still a number of unanswered questions. So tread carefully if you intend to use your competitors' trade marks in AdWords or metatags.

In addition to the issues discussed in this chapter, there have been many other areas that have attracted litigation, such as Google's suggestive search text field, which can be damaging where a brand has had bad publicity and does not want the details brought to the attention of searchers each time they perform a search on Google on its name. Google Maps has raised privacy issues, and the initiative to make books searchable has resulted in copyright litigation. What is for sure is that business online will continue to take place in an environment where both the law and technology are changing at a rapid pace.

Chapter 10: Key take-home messages

■ If you bid on others' trade mark names on AdWords make sure the ads don't confuse consumers into believing they emanate from the trade mark owner's business.

■ If someone is advertising on your trade mark name, consider whether their ad suggests an economic link with you, or is vague as to the origin of goods and services.

■ Beware of assuming your descriptive URL means you own trade mark rights over a particular descriptive keyword.

■ If you don't want your ads to appear on cybersquatters' web pages, opt out of Google's AdSense program when you use AdWords.

■ Protect your brand by regularly searching on your brand name to see if anyone is bidding on your name in an objectionable way.

Chapter 11

Essential points to know before licensing your products and services

'Intellectual Property is the oil of the 21st century' Mark Getty

Intellectual property licensing covers a multitude of possible business arrangements that enable you to make money from your knowledge, ideas, creative output, reputation, patents, trade marks, designs, and so on. The type of IP you own will determine the most suitable licensing option for commercialising it.

Your process, service or product will be identified by a trade mark name and other signs. It might also comprise a design that you have registered or been able to protect with a patent. Alternatively, your IP may be a copyright work. The contractual provisions that should be included in your licence agreement depend to some extent on the IP you are licensing.

Licensing enables you to keep your IP while granting others the right to use it under the terms of the licensing contract. Intellectual property licensing takes on different forms in different industries. For instance, publishing, music, cosmetics and pharmaceutical businesses all have their own issues and considerations to take into account. Let's look at how this will work in our example business, TTMC.

Gavin plans to grow his business by licensing others to offer his coaching methodology. These licensed practitioners will also sell his products and earn substantial commission on the sale price. His suite of offerings will include the following:

1. Various talks, which will be available to organisations or individuals. These might include giving advanced tips and imparting a broader understanding of his methodology, with topics such as improving organisational productivity and performance; mastering the basics; managing projects and priorities.

2. Coaching services, which will take the form of coaching assessments delivered on-site or virtually.

3. Trainer certification, which will enable experienced corporate trainers to deliver the methodology to staff within their organisations, with the aim of boosting performance, confidence and innovation of staff.

4. Consultancy, such as bespoke offerings created for different organisations to teach the methodology and align it with their corporate strategy and vision.

5. Online learning centre. This will be subscription based and initially will be offered to support implementation of the methodology for clients. It will also include online webinars, a multimedia library, discussion forum and starter training as well as refresher series.

6. Products such as audio CDs and software tools to run on platforms like Microsoft Outlook and systems for use on Macs, iPhone, or iPad or any other software that developers want to build in partnership with Gavin's business, such as downloads, books, videos and various planners and guides.

7. The new desk accessory to facilitate time management.

Licensing will enable Gavin to retain ownership of his intellectual property and effectively sell it on at the same time.

In this chapter, we'll look at some key considerations when commercialising your IP through licensing.

Why license: what are the advantages and the risks?

One advantage of licensing is that it enables you to grow your business more quickly, as your brand will be able to reach markets it could not otherwise access so soon or so widely. Licensing provides a cheaper and easier way to scale the business than growing it organically by using your own resources.

Expanding your business using your own resources requires staff and funding to deal with the workload in your immediate target market, and so the costs entailed in offering services to a new country might not be a viable option for you. However, another party may already have the staff and resources available within your target market and be readily able to handle the workload, allowing you to reach markets further afield.

Gavin would like to appoint one licensee per foreign territory to deliver the service element of his methodology in return for royalties, while the products will be sold directly from London. Licensees would order products from London if they sell any to their clients.

Although Gavin appreciates that he will make less profit than if he exploited a market alone and did not have to share the revenues, there are clear advantages to using licensed practitioners as a way to expand.

He believes there will be a demand for his training and approval process, and he will be able to charge for this, so he will earn fees from training licensed practitioners. If he were to expand his business by employing staff to deliver his methodology, he could ultimately make more money but would need substantial capital to finance that business model. By going down the licensing route he will be able to have different levels of practitioner, some of whom could go on to become 'master practitioners' with additional privileges and access to his know-how.

Registering his trade mark is important in order for Gavin to secure his brand and protect his methodology. It will also make it easier for him to protect his reputation and ensure that licensees observe key branding principles.

Franchising

Franchising is another type of licensing arrangement that is common in the service sector, where there is a proven business format that franchisees can buy into. It's a popular way to scale a business – think McDonald's, Subway, Coffee Republic, and so on.

The chocolate company Thorntons describes franchising as 'a working relationship between you and Thorntons in which we commit to do "things" for you and you for us'. Generally the brand owner, or franchisor, will provide training, know-how and other support along with permission to use the brand. In exchange, the franchisee fronts the initial capital for their business, helps to promote the brand and also pays a licence fee.

Managerial involvement is an important consideration when establishing a franchise. For example, if I decided to visit a branch of McDonald's while on a trip abroad, it would be because I already knew the brand and would expect service similar to that I'm familiar with at home. If I were disappointed in the service I received, this would be damaging to the McDonald's brand generally, not just to the particular outlet which delivered the poor service.

For this reason, quality control is exerted in every franchising deal, but maintaining standards can be a challenge. The very process of adapting a product or service to suit local needs can be detrimental to the overall brand, because making the product or service more suitable for local people will not necessarily please visitors. Non-franchise licensing agreements typically don't allow for such a level of managerial involvement.

Finding potential licensees

Before embarking on a licensing venture, think about how you will select the companies to whom you license your products or services. Whether you target them, or they approach you, it's important to understand the risks of the particular licence arrangement you are contemplating so you can manage them effectively. Considerations should include:

■ **the nature of the licensee company and its own products**

■ **the company's size and resources**

■ **the technical expertise of the company**

■ **the company's distribution capabilities.**

There are companies who offer services to help in the process of identifying suitable licensees, but think about what you could achieve yourself. Engaging professional help to find licensees or joint venture partners can be expensive and you may be better placed to do it yourself as you have a strong understanding of your own offering and the market.

Whether you seek out potential licensees yourself, or they come to you, it pays to have taken time to research in advance which businesses would benefit from your offering, and why, so you can be clear about your selection criteria.

Things to consider when selecting a licensee company:

■ **Consider the potential licensee's business model and resources, and estimate what it will cost them to take up your offering.**

- **When licensing a service, consider what will be involved for the licensee when it comes to delivery of your methodology.**

- **If you are licensing software, will the licensee need to spend time training staff? If the cost is likely to be high, then it's best to focus on larger businesses that are able to cope with the initial outlay.**

- **When licensing a product that will be resold, thereby earning you royalties, an important factor to consider is the reach of the potential licensee, such as how many names and addresses are on their list.**

To secure a deal, you might offer exclusivity, appointing only a single licensee. (An exclusive licence means you yourself may not exploit the IP in that locality, or indeed at all, depending on the basis on which you granted exclusivity. It's therefore important that the agreement safeguards your position in the event that the licensee does not live up to expectations).

Where a company has a background in striking licensing deals, they are more likely to be receptive to your approach. Many large companies who license products regularly will have a department dedicated to this activity. So if Gavin wants to license his potentially patentable desk accessory, he should establish whether there is a set procedure that a particular company uses for this process. And if his pitch is rejected, he should learn from this and ask for honest feedback. This will give him invaluable information about how to market the product more attractively next time.

On the other hand, if you have built up a brand name, the licensing deal might be for the other party to deliver a related product under your brand, such as software tailored to cater for your time management methodology. A successful fashion designer might license a perfume manufacturer to create a perfume range for its label. Sometimes, if you have a successful product or brand, the other party might want to license the right to sell your product under their own brand name. For example, Twiggy recently produced a range of clothes designs for Marks and Spencer.

Similarly, a well-known brand may lend its name to the other party. For example, a cook brand such as Nigella Lawson might license a seller of utensils and crockery to use her name on its products.

Extending your brand to related or completely different products raises a number of issues, as discussed in Chapter 3. But brand extensions that involve licensing your products or services to different categories could fail if the extension was inappropriate. For instance, Harley Davidson perfume proved to be an extension too far. And despite the fact that Virgin has been able to apply its brand to records, financial services, airlines and a variety of other products and services, it failed in its bid to extend its brand to colas.

Co-branding

Another way of making money from your IP is to engage in a joint venture, such as a co-branding exercise.

One successful example of this is the partnership between McDonald's and Disney. By supplying toys to McDonald's for inclusion in their Happy Meals, Disney was able to reach its target market of children and their parents very effectively. McDonald's was in turn able to offer free gifts, which attracted more custom for its meals. These types of partnerships, between businesses that do not compete with each other, also serve to substantially increase the visibility of each brand. The arrangement works for both parties because they offer complementary services targeting a similar list of prospective customers.

An example of co-branding would be if Gavin partners with someone who develops a Microsoft Outlook 'add on' that makes it easy to apply his methodology. In this way, the 'add on' developer comes to the attention of business organisations that are potential clients for its other software development services, while Gavin's company is able to offer a useful tool that simplifies the entire process of applying his methodology. Also, clients of the software developer may discover Gavin's products and services when they find out about the software developer's 'add on' software.

Owning intellectual property rights

Owning IP assets increases the value of a business, not only because assets can be transacted and sold like a plot of land, but also because they can be commercialised and exploited in order to generate money, and licensing is the way to do this.

Although it's possible to license unregistered rights – including names, copyrights, designs, and know-how – it is infinitely preferable to register rights where you can do so, before licensing them. It's also important to check that you have the necessary rights so that you are free to grant licences.

So, wherever the law provides a mechanism for securing rights, such as in names, designs, or copyrights, then make sure you secure them either by using appropriate contracts or by registering your rights. Then, in the event of any infringement, the remedies available to a licensee will be stronger, and this in turn increases the value of the licence.

Ownership of a trade mark is the foundation on which many types of licensing – such as sponsorship, ingredient branding, character merchandising and franchising – are based, and this puts you in a better position to exploit your brand. Manuals and other teaching aids that are used for training licensed practitioners can be protected by copyright, as can ownership of associated products.

Types of licences

Where your IP consists principally of expertise, then confidentiality may be a key way to protect your know-how, given that, during the course of operating the licence, the licensee will glean information about the market and other insights that you may want to protect from general disclosure. For this reason, you might want to have the licensee report back on certain points periodically.

Various safeguards are necessary to protect know-how information, depending on the type of business to which the licence relates. Enforcing confidential information provisions in foreign jurisdictions can be difficult and so this may be one consideration when deciding whom to appoint as your licensee.

Generally, a company whose core profitability stems from a trade secret or know-how will prefer an approach that lets it keep its trade secret or know-how to itself or within its own territory. On the other hand, if a company has a granted patent, it may be more inclined to grant licences for others to deliver the service or product.

Licence agreements

Intellectual property licensing initially began in the entertainment and fashion industries, but now there are licensing opportunities for all sorts of brands. Unfortunately, many trade mark owners don't take the proper precautions. If you don't license your mark properly you risk damage to your reputation or even loss of the mark.

For example, under trade mark law in many countries a trade mark owner can lose their rights if they allow third parties to use the mark without restriction. The way to avoid this is to make sure you carefully control the quality of the goods or services on which the mark is used and to limit your distributors' rights to sub-license the mark. This is the prime reason Gavin has decided not to give licensees the right to develop their own version of products, and he will restrict licensees to selling products that are manufactured for him in London. He will merely license the methodology of the service and, rather than allow his licensees to appoint sub-licensees, he will require any prospective assistants the licensees want to employ, to be authorised by himself.

The first consideration when approaching a licence agreement is to describe what is being licensed and to take account of the extent of your trade mark portfolio. What specific products or services are covered and in which geographic areas?

Who will be responsible for filing further trade marks, and who will bear the cost of these? As a general rule, it's important for you, the licensor, to keep responsibility for trade mark registration.

The licence will be for a specific period of time and may impose a number of conditions. In return the licensee agrees to pay you royalties and is willing to do so because you have something that's popular. As soon as your brand has the potential to attract customers, you have the potential to monetise it, and the structure of your licence is crucial to making the most of this opportunity. An early consideration will be whether it's necessary for you to grant exclusivity, which we'll look at below.

White labelling and affiliate schemes

One way in which it is possible to expand your reach is to offer white-labelling services, whereby you provide the service but someone else gets the credit for it.

Gavin's management consultancy service is not appropriate to offer on a white-label basis because the service component of the work will require a close working relationship between client and consultant. When his brand is sufficiently established he will be able to promote some of his online subscription services and his products on a white-label basis. This will enable other consultants offering time management solutions to benefit from some of Gavin's methodology without having to credit Gavin as the source.

An affiliate scheme is a different proposition. Here it is less important to have a brand so much as an offering that others feel they can either sell as an 'add on' to their products and services, or something they are willing to promote for a commission on sales. Gavin would be fully credited as the provider of the product or service.

Gavin wonders whether offering his videos, eBooks and other products to affiliates could considerably expand his reach as well as achieve more sales for his products. He decides to focus on licensing practitioners, and he will give them the equivalent rights that affiliates would have to sell his products. He is willing to share 50% of the profits from product sales with his licensees. For the time being, though, he does not see a value in allowing non-practitioners to promote and sell his products.

Exclusivity

It's important to have clarity on whether the licence is to be exclusive or non-exclusive in relation to each product category, territory, time period, or whatever else it is you're granting rights over.

An exclusive licence means that only your licensee may exploit the brand for the time period or throughout the territory specified in the contract. Even you won't have permission to do so. So, if you grant an exclusive licence for an extended period, say three years or so, be sure to include safeguards allowing you to terminate exclusivity if the licensee doesn't make adequate efforts to sell your product or service or fails to meet set turnover targets. If you don't want to exclude yourself, you could instead grant a sole licence. This allows for just one licensee in a given territory, but also permits you to compete.

Be aware that under English law, sole and exclusive licences are different rights, as described above. While you might hear of 'sole and exclusive' as one entity in licences in other jurisdictions, this doesn't apply in the UK.

Subject to certain constraints under EU law on free movement of goods and services, licences can be created in any number of product categories and territories. This means your licensee can tap into a wider global brand than it could otherwise afford to purchase outright. On the other hand, you as licensor derive a licence fee by way of a royalty. Such fees are generally based on a percentage of sales, but each deal can set whatever payment mechanism it wishes and there are no hard and fast rules.

Registration issues

Your trade mark licence should be registered with the Trade Marks Registry to ensure that losses of your licensees are taken into account when seeking compensation for infringement of your rights, or to allow exclusive licensees to take legal action in their own name.

Trade marks come to an end only if you fail to use them as registered or fail to renew them, or if they are directly challenged by another party. As they can potentially last forever, they can be a great investment. In contrast, patents and designs have a limited life.

Conclusion

Once you have a clear understanding of the objective behind the licensing arrangement and the markets you intend to reach, it's possible to arrive at a variety of creative solutions for exploiting your IP. As the brand owner, you should be the registered proprietor of the trade mark, not your distributor or licensee. So it's important to register your trade mark internationally. If you don't do this and the trade marks are registered in the name of licensees or distributors rather than in your name, you should insist on transferring those registrations into the name of the brand owner. The proprietor of the trade mark should be the owner of the goodwill and reputation in the mark in question, and so both rights should be vested in the same person. Generally, only the registered proprietor can begin trade mark infringement proceedings (though if transactions are registered correctly, licensees may also do so under certain circumstances). Wherever you use your mark, or where you manufacture, distribute or license a third party to promote it, is where you should consider registering the mark ultimately.

Chapter 11: Key take-home messages

■ Licensing provides a cheaper and easier way to scale your business than growing it organically by using your own resources, and gives you access to wider markets.

■ When seeking out a licensee, be clear about your selection criteria, taking into account the potential licensee's business model and available resources.

■ Make sure that any licensing agreement safeguards your position in the event that the licensee does not live up to expectations.

■ Where you can, register your trade mark before entering into a licensing deal, otherwise you risk damage to your reputation or even loss of the mark.

Part Four

Brand Protection

Chapter 12

Securing your brand assets through trade mark registration

'A brand name is more than a word.
It is the beginning of a conversation' Lexicon

Trade marks are identifiers. According to the legal definition in the UK's Trade Marks Act 1994 a trade mark is 'any sign capable of being represented graphically which is capable of distinguishing goods or services of one undertaking from those of other undertakings'.

As we saw earlier, signs that are typically registered as trade marks are names, logos, and straplines. The name is the primary sign because it's how we identify a brand. Even when a brand has a very distinctive visual identity, such as Nike's famous 'swoosh' logo or Coca-Cola's distinctive bottle shape, we invariably refer to it by its name. Registering the name is therefore your first priority.

Although an essential function of trade marks is to designate the origin of goods or services so that consumers can reliably find products and services, when it comes to a registered trade mark, not all names have the same value.

We know that an effective name for a trade mark is one that is distinctive such that there are very few similar names on the registers. It's the equivalent of owning a secure house. Similarly, having a weak name is like owning a house that you can easily break into, as it makes you more vulnerable to competitors stealing your market share. It will also be expensive for you to enforce your rights against competitors.

In theory, it's possible to register almost any name, even a descriptive one, if you combine it with a logo in your application to register the trade mark. However, such a registration will protect the logo, and does not give you exclusive rights over the name element of the mark. You would only get exclusive rights over a name if you register it on its own without adding a logo in the same application.

Zumba

Zumba is an effective name from a legal point of view. Registering it as a trade mark means that anyone who wanted to provide Zumba dance classes or use the name would need to have the company's permission first.

Had the owners of this dance fitness programme given it a descriptive name like 'New Latin Dance' they would have found it both expensive and difficult to stop others using similar names. They would also be in a weaker position to monetise their creation.

If the owners of Zumba had delayed in applying to register the name, they might have failed to secure trade mark rights at a later date due to the fact that Zumba rapidly gained widespread popularity and could therefore be deemed too descriptive a name to trademark.

Descriptiveness is a bar to registration

Cases involving Elvis Presley, Diana, Princess of Wales, and Sir Alex Ferguson memorabilia have illustrated that it's not possible to register trade marks when the fame of the individuals is so widespread that the mark has become merely descriptive. Such marks would need to have been registered before the person became a celebrity.

Similarly, Microsoft's delay in applying to register the name of its Windows operating system nearly lost it the chance to secure a registration.

Case study: Microsoft

Microsoft used to pay less attention to its trade marks than to its patents, until it almost lost the opportunity to protect its Windows mark. Although Microsoft first introduced its Windows software in 1985, it did not file a trade mark application until 1990. By then Windows was so well known that the US Patent and Trademark Office (USPTO) initially rejected Microsoft's trade mark application on the grounds that the Windows mark was 'merely descriptive' in relation to computer software.

By 1990, many people associated the Windows interface with the way in which the software displayed the user's desktop. Microsoft kept arguing its case, and fought hard to secure a registration. Eventually in 1995, the Trademark Office granted the Windows trade mark application. In the meantime, Microsoft had continued to gain market share for its Windows software, and it would have been a huge blow to its marketing plans if the trade mark had not been granted.

The delay in filing an application meant Microsoft nearly destroyed the brand equity it had created in the early years of its initial introduction of its Windows products. During these years, Microsoft was gaining ever-increasing brand recognition of its software product. If the USPTO had ultimately refused to issue the Windows trade mark, Microsoft would have ended up with virtually no proprietary rights to the 'Windows' name. Introducing a new brand name at that time would have put Microsoft in a very different competitive position. Would Microsoft be where it is today if it did not brand its game-changing, mid-1990s product as 'Windows 95'?

Following that error with the Windows trade mark, Microsoft has changed its approach and is always alive to the need to brand and trade-mark its Internet platform products.

The value of trade marks

Many technology-orientated companies, especially start-ups, often don't recognise the make-or-break value that a trade mark can have on their ability to make inroads into a crowded market. Rather, these often cash-strapped companies believe that if they are going to spend any money on IP protection, then that money should go towards protecting their technology by way of a patent. Microsoft's near miss with its Windows trade mark, as well as its subsequent aggressive stance toward protecting its trade marks, copyrights and trade secrets, should be a warning for other companies to prioritise appropriately.

Case study: Twitter

The social networking service Twitter is another example of a company that nearly did not secure a trade mark over the word 'Tweet'.

Twitter had to go to extreme lengths to secure Tweet as a trade mark, by buying out another company's registration which incorporated the word Tweet. Once the word was in such widespread use, it would have jeopardised Twitter's ability to secure its own registration over the word.

Small businesses should not draw comfort from the happy endings for the likes of Microsoft. Without the resources of a company like Microsoft, Apple, Google or Twitter, it would be impossible to extricate yourself from the kind of trade mark problems these brands have sometimes had to address. So it's doubly important for SMEs to get it right.

Choice of name and vetting

It's not widely understood that the choice of name is itself a legal matter. Not all names are equally effective from a legal standpoint. Indeed, some names are far easier to protect than others. Bear in mind, too, that not all names are capable of functioning as a trade mark, as we saw in Chapters 2 and 3.

If you are intending to have a brand that you can use globally, it's desirable to establish its availability on the registers of other countries. This will alert you to the possibility of whether you could be infringing on other people's rights, and if it's necessary to make a change it is far easier to do it straight away.

The name you settle on could be in the form of a domain name such as lastminute.com, or it could be your company name. All sorts of names can be registered – for example, a band or group name, the name of an orchestra or venue, a label, a book or film title. And if, for instance, you were making a film and wanted to produce merchandise such as mugs, T-shirts and costumes, you should consider registering the names of characters from the film.

Other possible brand names are the name of your restaurant, magazine, software program, award or charity. Even a building or ship name may be registered as your trade mark, as can your own name as long as it's not a common name like Gavin Brown.

Gavin has shortlisted a few names and intends to use the name, once all legal checks are completed, for all his products and services, taking a house brand approach.

Planning ahead

When creating a new brand, it can be confusing to know the order in which to do things – such as choosing a suitable name, registering domain names, incorporating and designing logos. People tend to do all these things and then only at the end of a branding project do they turn to a lawyer to protect the brand. This is the wrong way to go about it and leaves little scope to benefit from the expertise of a brand lawyer in helping you to pick a legally effective name. Once you've invested in your initial choice name by having a brand identity created around it, you are likely to drop the name only if a significant problem is identified.

Gavin Brown wants to go about choosing his new brand name properly, which is why he has put forward a shortlist of three to six names as alternatives to The Time Management Company. Among the shortlist is the acronym TTMC, although he is not sure he wants to go with that option even if it is available.

He knows better than to get too attached to any one name. He has not yet invested in a domain or a logo design and wants to clear the name internationally first before buying domain names. He also intends to file a trade mark before engaging branding services.

Before finalising his choice of name Gavin did some Google searches. This reduces the risk of picking a name that belongs to someone else. He eliminated many of the names he had initially thought of after doing some online searches and finding that others were using the name. His brand lawyers had suggested he keep a record of his search results to send to them with his queries and thoughts. Such preliminary online checks will save unnecessary disappointment and expense.

If you find that someone in another country is using the same name, it doesn't necessarily present an insurmountable problem. Does that country matter to you, and is the other party using the name in a competing business? If not, then you can still consider using that name.

If nothing is found on Google, that's a good sign but by no means conclusive that the name is available to use. There could be many reasons why you may not find evidence of uses of a mark online even though it may be registered, and unavailable for you to adopt as a trade mark. For example, not all websites are search-engine friendly, and not all products and services are promoted by name online. Someone could have registered a mark but not yet begun to use it, as it's possible to register a name up to five years before using it.

So you will still need a professional to search the trade mark registers. The scope of protection afforded by a trade mark is not limited to the same name, but extends to similar names. So, whether the name you want to register is apparently available or has been taken, it's sensible to get a legal opinion before assuming you can or can't use a name.

> As it was important to Gavin to be able to register his new name as a domain and company name, he has also checked the availability of these so he can register them once the legal checks are completed.

Changing descriptive names

As descriptive names are not eligible for trade mark registration, it's quite common for companies which started out with descriptive names to rebrand when they want to scale their business, as Gavin is doing.

> Although Gavin is considering using the acronym TTMC as one of his brand name options, along the lines of Business Networking International, which became BNI, it is not his first choice of name. Many brands, including HSBC, BA and BT, which rebranded for similar reasons, have adopted acronyms, but Gavin wants a more powerful brand name than a set of initials. He thinks initials are not very memorable or capable of suggesting what the business does. However, that may not matter as he will be asking his branding agency to create a slogan for his business that incorporates the words 'Time Management.'

Borderline descriptive

While it's possible for a brand lawyer to give an opinion on whether or not a name is too descriptive for trade mark registration, when it clearly falls at either end of the descriptive scale it can sometimes be difficult to predict how the Trade Marks Registry will assess a name that's borderline descriptive.

One disadvantage of choosing a borderline descriptive name is that if the registry objects to it, you waste time and money until a final outcome is reached, and in the meantime you have to plan your affairs in a climate of uncertainty. This uncertainty will be multiplied if the mark is to be registered in other countries, as each country will have its own view of whether the mark is within the bounds of acceptability.

In view of the discretionary nature of trade marks, there is an element of luck as to which examiner handles your trade mark, or which hearing officer handles any appeal. So you could find yourself in a situation where your mark is registered in one country but not in another. Added to which it would be more costly to protect your brand if you used a borderline descriptive name.

Acquired distinctiveness

Descriptive marks such as Philadelphia cheese make it to the registers only because they become distinctive over time through extensive advertising and long-standing use.

To prove to the Trade Marks Registry that a mark has become distinctive, it is necessary to provide external proof of distinctiveness. Trade marks registries in different countries will require proof that meets the standards acceptable to them, before deciding whether a descriptive mark has become distinctive within their own country. The proof they will require generally involves establishing that the name is used as an identifier by the public, rather than that people simply recognise the mark.

The expense of producing evidence to persuade registries across the world that a given mark has become distinctive in each of the respective countries should not be underestimated, so it's not advisable to choose a descriptive name on the off chance that it may acquire distinctiveness.

Each country will require evidence to show that the mark has become distinctive there. In practice, decisions from trade marks registries are not always predictable or consistent. This means that marks with descriptive elements will always cost a lot more both to register and to defend.

In conclusion, whether you would like to register a mark on the basis that it's become distinctive, or would like to register a borderline descriptive mark, it's important to go into it knowing that it will be more costly.

It can also work out expensive where a mark leans towards the descriptive end of the scale of registrable trade marks. The fact that it has been accepted for registration in the UK or EU does not mean that it will also be accepted in other countries. You may need to factor into your budget the cost of engaging Australian or US lawyers, for example, if your mark is considered insufficiently distinctive to merit registration in those countries.

Unregistered rights

Although it is not necessary to register a name as a trade mark in order to use it, the only effective way to secure exclusive rights to a name is to register it as a trade mark.

Remember that the trade mark registers are public, as is the Land Registry. Therefore, others are 'on notice' that you have registered rights in the name. There is a similar doctrine of notice of rights in land. This means that if you are using a name without registering it, you are inviting problems, such as running the risk of other people starting businesses using the same name as yours. If you've registered your rights and someone else begins using the same name, they are automatically in the wrong because the law regards them as having notice of your rights. On the other hand, where your rights are not registered, the unsatisfactory solutions to subsequent infringement problems that the courts might reach (more about this in Chapter 15) are another reason not to let this happen.

Failure to register a name that you want to build your brand identity around is a poor decision and a mistake that only inexperienced small businesses make.

Even in countries that base priority of trade mark rights on a 'first-to-use' basis (as happens in the United States), it's important to register trade marks in order to put third parties on notice of your rights in the name. In the US, if you don't register a trade mark, your 'first-to-use' trade mark rights extend only to the territories in which the trade mark has actually been adopted and used. Registration on the Principal Register of the US Patent and Trademark Office (USPTO), however, provides a presumption of an exclusive right to use the registered mark throughout the United States, even if the mark is not actually adopted and used in every state.

Classifications

Before registering a trade mark, it's important to be clear about your immediate and longer-term plans because trade marks are registered for specific business activities. So choosing the classes in which your business provides, or intends to provide goods, or services is the first step to laying claim to the scope of your rights in a name.

If you don't register your rights adequately, the danger is that someone else could register the same name or a similar name for an area of your business that you have not included in your registration.

Knowing what niche you want to occupy helps in determining which of the 45 classes of goods and services are relevant for your trade mark application, bearing in mind that it's possible to register a name well before you intend to use it.

The trade mark classes and the way you draft your application determine the boundaries around your mark, just as fences stake out the territorial rights in a plot of land.

There are literally thousands of descriptions within each class, so it is even possible for two businesses with the same name to register within the same class. For example AA is registered as a word mark by both American Airlines and the Automobile Association in class 39 covering transportation services.

Two businesses can co-exist in this way either because their activities are so different that consumer confusion is unlikely, or because the businesses have come to an agreement between themselves, as Apple computers did with the Apple Records label.

Once you get your trade mark certificate, you have exclusive rights to use the mark in relation to the business categories included in your certificate.

The registration will also give you a certain level of protection over overlapping areas, but this is a grey area and might involve litigation in order to determine this, so it's best not to rely on it. If you specifically need a particular category, then register for that category too.

In conclusion, it is more cost-effective to include all the necessary classes at the outset. Otherwise, other parties might register to use the same or a similar name in the areas of activity in which you did not register, and lock you out from extending your brand in ways you might intend to extend it in future. For example, if you register in the category that covers clothing, might you also want to extend the brand to cover cosmetics?

Choosing your territory

An early decision involves where you will trade and under what brand. If you intend to use the same name worldwide, you will need to check its availability internationally and then register a trade mark, country by country, focusing on your most important markets first.

Once you've decided where you will be trading, the next question is whether to apply for a UK trade mark or a Community trade mark (CTM) that is valid across the European Union.

Registering a trade mark with the UK Intellectual Property Office gives you rights in the UK, whereas a CTM gives you rights in all 27 EU countries including the UK. As a CTM application covers the whole of the EU in a single application, it's the most cost-effective choice if you do business in more than one European country. The overall price to register a CTM is lower than registering in two EU countries. It takes at least five months from the date a CTM is filed for the certificate to come through, depending on the registry's workload.

If you apply for a CTM and someone has already registered a similar trade mark in any one of the 27 EU countries, they may oppose your application. If this happens, your entire application is delayed pending the outcome and would be refused if the trade mark owner is successful or refuses to come to an arrangement with you. This is what happened with Google's Gmail CTM application.

Case study: Google

Google's application to register the name 'Gmail' was successfully opposed by the owner of an earlier trade mark registered in Germany. Similarly, the existence of a right in the UK meant that Google had to use the name googlemail.com in the UK.

Google's failure to check whether it could use the name before launching its service resulted in nearly a decade of litigation before both cases were satisfactorily settled, with Google paying undisclosed sums of money to secure the rights in the UK and Germany.

If you don't have the same financial resources as Google to buy your way out of trouble, you can avoid problems by having trade mark searches undertaken before you finally settle on a name.

Costs

The official fees for registering a UK trade mark are lower than for registering a CTM. (The current official fees are given on Azrights.com/trademarks/fees.)

Once an application is filed, no refunds are given if it fails, and only limited amendments of the application are possible.

Trade marks can last indefinitely, because a mark may be renewed every ten years by paying a further fee and completing a short form.

International branding

If you sell online and have customers in different countries, bear in mind that you will be using your mark in those other territories too.

The law has always been slow to catch up with new technology and developments, and nowhere is this more evident than on the Internet. The territorial nature of trade marks sits poorly with the global nature of Internet business. The current international trade mark system is designed for a very different business environment, one that's more suited to the pocket of well-resourced, well-funded multinationals that gradually move into new markets.

Nevertheless, if you do want to be able to use the same brand name in all countries in which you might trade, then you need to take a wider view and check the availability of the name in a number of other countries and register as and when you acquire customers in a country. Otherwise, you could be infringing on the trade mark rights of local competitors and potentially lose a lucrative market if you have to block sales to that country.

International priority protection

Trade marks share some similarities worldwide even though each country's laws will differ, having originated from different philosophical and legal traditions. While the details of the law differ from country to country, there are international initiatives that make it possible to secure trade mark protection on an international level.

The registration system has emerged from such international initiatives and gives you a priority right for up to six months to apply for trade mark protection in other countries covering the same mark.

So once you've filed an application for a UK or CTM trade mark, provided you go on to file for trade mark protection in your desired territories within six months of filing your UK or CTM application, you may claim priority over third parties who may have filed an application in those countries in the meantime.

So, this is a time-limited right that is triggered by the first filing of an application, and is granted by virtue of international treaties between countries, to which most countries have signed up.

This is not completely foolproof, as we'll see below, but is a good enough basis for protecting a mark in jurisdictions that matter to you without having to incur the costs of international filing as soon as you start up with a new name.

'First to file' or 'first to use'?

Many countries determine priority of trade mark rights on a 'first-to-file' for registration basis rather than on a 'first-to-adopt-and-use' basis.

Some first-to-file trade mark systems include China, France, Germany, Japan, and Spain. The United States is a first-to-adopt-and-use country.

In first-to-file countries, prior use is not a prerequisite to registering a trade mark. Also, in first-to-file countries, use of the mark (without a registration) will not provide priority trade mark rights.

So there is literally a race to the trade marks offices in those countries with a first-to-file for registration system, and prompt applications for registrations are critical for protection of trade marks in those countries.

Bear this in mind when relying on the six-month priority right for international registration. Consider whether you want to reduce the risks by filing for protection immediately in any first-to-file country that represents a significant market for your brand.

Madrid system applications

The Madrid system provides a simple way to register a trade mark in countries which are members of an international system known as the Madrid Protocol. (You can find an up-to-date list of countries within the Madrid system at www.azrights.com/Madrid.)

At the time of writing, a number of countries are not party to the Madrid scheme. For example, Hong Kong, Canada and South Africa are outside the system. To trade mark in these countries it is necessary to engage local agents to file directly in their local trade mark registries.

There are many advantages of registering through the Madrid Protocol in terms of ease of administration, cost savings and flexibility.

A Madrid application uses a single form listing all the countries in which you wish to apply for trade mark protection. The classes are specified (and cannot include any that were not listed in your initial UK or CTM application).

The costs can quickly mount if you need to register in a number of classes and countries. In practice, if you are on a budget you will have to decide which markets matter to you the most, and then register in them, leaving other countries for a later round of registration.

The trade mark registries of the countries specified in your application then have 18 months in which to raise any objections to your application. If none are raised, your application is deemed accepted.

Once you file an application under the Madrid system, if objections are raised in any given country, your mark will not be accepted there unless you are able to overcome the objections. Overcoming the objections would entail engaging the services of a local lawyer in that particular country as your UK lawyers would not have 'rights of audience' to correspond with the foreign registry.

However, unlike CTMs, if your application fails in any of your desired countries, it will still be acceptable in other countries unless there are valid objections raised against it in any of those countries too.

One point to be aware of is that if your international trade mark was based on a UK or CTM application, and your UK or CTM application was cancelled for any reason, it would have an impact on your whole international trade mark portfolio.

The important role that the initial application plays in your subsequent international trade mark ownership is a good reason to do some thorough investigations before making the application, and to have it professionally drafted for you.

Why registering in other territories is important

Two cases which illustrate the importance of filing trade mark applications in other countries as your business begins to expand are outlined below.

The first case involves Raxisia (a fictitious name to protect the identity of the parties).

Raxisia

This e-commerce site had been selling its products in the United States for more than eight years without having registered a trade mark there. A competitor then set up a bricks and mortar shop in the United States selling similar products and also called itself Raxisia. The original Raxisia company was alerted to this when publicity surrounding the new shop was spotted by one of its existing customers who emailed to congratulate it on its new venture in California.

Raxisia had to engage lawyers to file a trade mark application in the United States. After hefty costs and legal correspondence, the US attorneys successfully secured a US registration for Raxisia. This was achieved because of the numerous customers that the company had in the United States and in California. US trade mark rules gave the original Raxisia prior rights in the name.

The company could have avoided the hefty legal fees if it had registered its mark in the United States as soon as it began selling its products there.

This second case illustrates how the territorial system of trade marks does not sit well with the global nature of Internet business.

Plenty of Fish v. Plenty More Fish

Plentyoffish.com was a well-established online dating site for many years when PlentyMoreFish.com set up a competing online business based in the UK, and applied to register a trade mark in the UK.

Plenty of Fish wanted to stop Plenty More Fish from creating customer confusion and benefiting from the reputation it had built up online. It decided to oppose Plenty More Fish's UK trade mark application.

The only reason Plenty More Fish was able to set up a competing service using a similar name was that it based its business in the UK and applied to register a trade mark in the UK. The global village environment of the Internet, and its lack of territorial boundaries, was to its advantage because it could divert some of Plenty of Fish's business to itself (simply due to the confusion between the two similar names).

Had both businesses been based within the same territorial borders, it would have amounted to passing off and trade mark infringement to set up a competing business to that of an established player, by using a similar name. However, as Plenty of Fish was an Internet business, the question of whether Plenty of Fish had rights in the UK to prevent Plenty More Fish from registering a trade mark turned on whether it had customers in the UK. If it did have customers there, it would have had 'earlier rights' in the UK and may have been successful in opposing Plenty More Fish's trade mark application and prevent it using a similar name.

However, as the company did not have any subscribers in the UK, it was unable to prevent Plenty More Fish from using a similar name online and registering a UK trade mark.

By contrast, in the Raxisia example above, the company did have customers in the United States and so was able to prevent the local shop from trading off its goodwill.

Non-word signs

Some businesses use logos, colour (e.g. orange as in the phone company Orange), shapes (e.g. the iconic Coca-Cola bottle) and musical melody (e.g. 118 118 for the insurance company Direct Line) as signs by which their products and services are identified. It's even been known for smells to be registered as a trade mark, such as the smell of grass for tennis balls.

While any sign capable of graphical representation – including designs, letters, numerals, packaging, colours, sounds, smells, and shapes – may be registered as a trade mark, it may be more difficult for such signs to be accepted for registration. It's only famous businesses whose non-name signs have become so well known that the general population can identify them simply by a shape or a colour, who are able to succeed in shape and colour registrations.

Logos

Another sign that businesses tend to register as a trade mark is their logo. For example, Nike's famous swoosh is registered as a trade mark, in addition to its brand name.

Every business will probably secure two registrations, one over its brand name and another over its logo. If they use the two together, they may also register a third combined mark, and if they have a strapline that is sometimes used with the name or logo, it would be appropriate to register them all together too. So, in practice most businesses are likely to need several trade mark registrations.

If you have to choose between registering the name or the logo, then the name is the one to trade mark because it's the primary way in which consumers will identify a brand.

Logos do have some protection under copyright, as we saw in Chapter 5, and design registration is also available in the first year.

Whose name should you choose for registration?

A question that often comes up for a business is in whose name should the IP be registered? Should the registration be in the name of the owner, or in the name of the company, and if there are several companies in the group, the question is which one should own the rights? The answer is to register in the name of the person with goodwill or reputation in the brand.

It's important to take a consistent approach to the identity of the proprietor when registering trade marks. So, where there is a group company structure, ideally all your applications should be in the name of the parent or holding company. This way you avoid the risk of trade marks being in the name of a company that has been transferred out of your group or has been dissolved!

Why not do the registration yourself?

A serious downside in doing your own legal work, without professional help, is that you may not do the job correctly. You get no insight into whether a name is suitable for registration or whether you may be infringing on someone else's rights by registering a name.

A ticking time bomb

As trade marks protect the owner against competitors using similar names, the fact that you have secured a trade mark registration does not prevent another trade mark owner who considers you to be infringing on its rights from challenging you at some future date. The trade mark owner may ignore you while you're an insignificant business, but if you do become a threat they could challenge your registration later. By then you may have a solid business, and be reliant on the income. Having to rebrand and lose an identity that's become successful could be devastating, as we'll discuss in Chapter 15.

An example of how a registration can be challenged is illustrated in the case of the food company Love Bites.

Waist Watchers

Love Bites registered a trade mark for Waist Watchers in 2005 and began selling Waist Watchers sandwiches. The slimming group Weight Watchers expressed its displeasure to Love Bites in a letter, but when Waist Watchers carried on, Weight Watchers decided Love Bites were too unimportant to worry about and ignored Waist Watchers' registration.

However, the company later changed its mind and commenced legal proceedings, arguing that the similarity of the marks and products would result in consumer confusion. It argued that Waist Watchers was taking unfair advantage of the reputation of the Weight Watchers' mark and might even damage its reputation.

Any brand lawyer would have been able to advise Waist Watchers that it was infringing on the Weight Watchers mark by using this name, regardless of the fact that it had secured a trade mark for the name. Waist Watchers will now have to rebrand. This case illustrates the importance of taking proper advice early on, and not assuming that a trade mark registration protects your business from infringing on others' rights. The only reliable way to assess the risks is to conduct a professional search and assess existing registrations to consider whether use of a particular mark is open to challenge by another trade mark.

If your use of a mark is challenged, then the trade mark owner may claim damages going back several years for trading off the goodwill of its name.

So with trade marks you're in dangerous territory when you pick a name that is similar to that of a competing trade mark owner, regardless of whether or not you are simply using the name as a domain name and whether or not you have a registered trade mark in the name.

Is the name legally effective and available?

A second downside to doing your own registration is that you do not get a legal opinion on the suitability of your name in relation to your business plans.

The question of whether a name is a good one from a trade mark perspective is rarely only about whether you can secure a registration for it. It's also about how easily competitors may get round your registration by using a confusingly similar name. What would be involved in enforcing rights in a particular name? Are you aware that some names involve far more litigation costs than others? These are all matters to take into account when settling on a name.

You may register just about any name if you try hard enough. Whether the trade mark certificate you obtain is worth the paper it's written on is another matter altogether, and it's always best to seek professional advice.

Professional indemnity

The third reason not to do your own legal work for something as important as your trade mark is that by using a lawyer you will be able to claim on their professional indemnity insurance should anything go wrong. It's unlikely that you could draft a trade mark application as effectively as a lawyer with years of experience, so why not get the job done professionally?

Although having a professional draft your trade mark application reduces the chance of an error occurring, it's still useful to have somebody to blame and claim from if things go wrong.

Remember, the reason you acquire an IP right is to own an asset and protect your brand against various eventualities such as unfair competition. Although securing your IP at the outset will cost money, it can cost you far more later on in lost opportunities or settling disputes if you don't go about it properly or you choose a legally ineffective name. Having IP rights gives a business more freedom, and the registration or contractual document is a form of insurance.

Conclusion

Registration is the way to own exclusive rights in a name, logo or tagline. In this chapter we saw some of the many pitfalls that await the unwary. I will pick up again on these issues in Chapter 15.

Chapter 12: Key take-home messages

■ It's inadvisable to use a name without registering it as a trade mark. Registration is the only effective way to secure exclusive rights in a name.

■ Be clear about your immediate and longer-term plans before registering your mark so as to ensure your mark is registered for all your intended business activities.

■ Take proper advice early on and don't assume that a trade mark registration protects your business from infringing on others' rights.

■ Acquiring IP rights gives a business more freedom, and the registration or contractual document acts as a form of insurance.

Chapter 13

How to use your trade marks to safeguard your brand

'It takes many good deeds to build a good reputation, and only one bad one to lose it'
Benjamin Franklin

It's necessary to look after your intellectual property rights such as trade marks, designs, patents, and your business reputation, in the same way that you would take care of your physical property.

You would protect your home against intruders by using locks on windows and your front door, and you'd mow your lawn and generally maintain the property to avoid having it fall into disrepair. Similarly, you need to protect your brand assets. It costs at least ten times as much to put matters right as it does to prevent problems caused by neglect.

There are a number of dos and don'ts to be aware of in order to safeguard your brand assets.

Correct use of the mark as registered

Once you have registered your mark, you should use the appropriate notices alongside it wherever you use the mark in order to indicate that it is a registered trade mark. By positioning the symbol ® next to the brand name, you alert the world to your rights in the mark.

However, 'TM' is the symbol to place next to your brand name before you register your mark, to let others know you are using the word in a trade mark sense. Designers who are creating a logo for your brand before you have registered your mark will, quite rightly, use the TM symbol. Ideally, you would have registered your trade mark before having branding work undertaken, so that your designers can use the ® symbol straight away and avoid the need to change it later. Once the trade mark is registered, it's more difficult to change the sign. For instance, shop signs are not so readily changed and this is a good reason to register your mark well before getting a sign designed.

In larger businesses it's commonplace to draw up guidelines on how to use the trade mark so that the logo is used consistently with the same typeface, graphics and configuration. Trade marks can be cancelled on the grounds of non-use, so if you register a logo or a combined word and logo mark, and then decide to change the logo at a later date, make sure you renew your registration to reflect the new logo.

Similarly, if you register a combined word and logo mark, you should avoid using the word and logo separately unless you also make separate registrations for the individual word and logo.

If you use your mark incorrectly, as outlined above, you are, in effect, using a new mark that is different from the one that appears in your trade mark certificate. This means that your registered mark won't protect you and could be revoked for non-use if a third party challenged it.

Lawyers commonly look for deficiencies in your position in the event that you claim their client is infringing your mark. If you aren't using your mark in the form in which it was registered, you leave yourself open to arguments that your mark is no longer valid. Your position is considerably weakened and, indeed, is in certain respects no better than if you had not registered your mark at all.

Use it or lose it

As it's possible to lose a trade mark for non-use in many jurisdictions, it's important to be strict about using the trade mark in the exact form in which it is registered. So, if you have registered a singular word, don't start using it in the plural unless you have also registered the plural version.

To get round this, you could always pluralise the generic term for your product, such as using 'Xerox copies' instead of 'Xeroxes'.

Similarly, avoid abbreviating, shortening or hyphenating your mark unless you have also registered those variations. For example, in addition to its full name, Marks and Spencer has registered M&S, but not Marks and Sparks, even though some people may refer to the company by the latter name. However, should Marks and Spencer decide to own 'Marks and Sparks' too, it should register that name separately.

Your stationery and any promotional sales material such as brochures or advertisements must also use the word as registered. This is good for marketing as well as trade mark purposes, as it helps consumers associate your trade mark with a particular product.

Whenever you are using your mark, for instance in your marketing literature, consider distinguishing it from the rest of the text by capitalising it or using different fonts or even putting it in quotes, for example BRAND X, Brand X, or 'Brand X'. This will help consumers to recognise the word as a brand name.

And don't forget to renew your trade mark, and each variation of it, every ten years.

Register for trade marks in other countries as you expand your brand

The case of *Plenty of Fish v. Plenty More Fish*, which we looked at in Chapter 12, shows how vulnerable an online business can be to unfair competition when it has not registered a trade mark and is unable to prove that it was the first company to use a name in the territory in question. Similarly, it cost the online e-commerce site Raxisia (discussed in Chapter 12) a lot of time and money in litigation fees when a competitor set up a physical shop in the in the same territory, selling very similar products and using the same name. It makes sense therefore to avoid the same fate by registering trade marks as you begin selling your products in other countries.

Gavin has already sold products to the United States, so he should look to register his mark there too. As his trading expands, so should his trade mark portfolio.

In certain countries – China, for example – where a large majority of counterfeit goods are produced, it's a good idea to have a defensive registration to prevent your manufacturer from registering your mark. As Gavin's desk accessory is to be manufactured in China, it's important that Gavin registers the trade mark there too.

If an overseas manufacturer were to register your mark it would be even more difficult and expensive to take remedial action, and in the meantime your goods would be blocked from leaving that country. In China, it's necessary to produce the trade mark certificate before exporting. Registration is therefore the smart course of action.

Review your registration periodically

Another important way in which to protect your mark is to review your registration periodically in case you need to register in other business classes.

Remember that people can legitimately sell goods and services using the same name as yours, provided there is no consumer confusion. For instance, the name Polo is registered to at least three famous companies, Volkswagen, Ralph Lauren and Nestlé, but for different goods – cars, clothing and confectionery.

Reviewing your registration gives you an opportunity to make sure you are not infringing on third parties' rights, and it also secures the rights you need so that others don't encroach on your mark. So, make sure you extend your registration in all the classes in which you provide goods and services.

Register your trade mark in other classes as you expand or fine-tune your niche

If you decide to expand your product range or start to offer new services, this is a sign that you may need to extend your trade mark registration to cover other classes. In fact, you should do this whenever you make any change in your business practice. For instance, a law firm might decide to narrow its niche from offering legal services to offering a particular type of legal service that intersects with a different industry, presenting it with a trade mark conflict which didn't exist before. Intellectual property services are provided by different professionals, so a general practice law firm may be able to co-exist with an intellectual property firm of patent and trade mark attorneys, but if it changed its focus from general practice to intellectual property services it could not co-exist with such a firm.

The time to consider your trade mark position is before you make any changes.

Remember that it's possible to infringe on someone else's trade mark rights and so you might need to rebrand for one particular activity. Trade marks should not be viewed as a one-time issue, and should be kept under constant review.

Beware of 'genericity'

If your mark initially starts out as distinctive but then loses its distinctiveness and becomes descriptive, or 'generic', this creates another situation where you could potentially lose your trade mark registration. 'Genericity' is a term used to refer to a mark that is synonymous with all versions of the product sold under that mark.

An example of when a mark can lose its distinctiveness and become generic is where people begin to use a trade mark as a verb or a noun, such as saying they are 'googling' or 'facebooking' instead of 'doing a Google search' or 'using Facebook'.

While it may be flattering for a brand to gain such recognition, this could be disastrous for its trade mark rights.

One way to reduce the risk is to use generic descriptors to clearly differentiate the trade mark and the product, such as by using 'Xerox copier' or 'Kleenex tissues', and ensuring that everyone else does likewise. This helps protect the brand name from genericity. You could also insert the word 'brand' into your marketing and advertising literature, to distinguish the presence of a trade mark, as in 'Hoover brand vacuum cleaners'.

Google's introduction of Google+ was accompanied by a rebranding exercise whereby long-standing products such as Picasa and Blogger became 'Google Photos' and 'Google Blogs'. By adding 'Google' and a generic descriptor to clearly differentiate the trade mark and the product in all its products and services, Google is effectively protecting its mark.

Traditionally, companies facing genericity have placed advertisements to educate the market in the use of their brand name, asking people to note the correct way to use their mark – such as, 'please use 'Xerox copier' or 'Kleenex tissues'.

Genericity can happen when a new invention is not given an alternative name, as happened with Aspirin. A way to avoid this problem is to consider giving a product two names at the outset: one to describe the product, and the other to act as your brand name. For instance, Aspirin used to be a trade marked name for a pain reliever medicine made of acetylsalicylic acid that was made by only one company. Now it is synonymous with that type of painkiller and is made by many companies. Had the original trade mark owner given the public an alternative name for that type of painkiller (for example, Aspirin could have been chosen as the name of the painkiller, while the brand name could have been something else, Forlief, say), it would still be benefiting from its invention under the brand name, long after its patents expired.

Many other once-famous marks are now only generic words and are no longer trade marks in certain countries, if at all. These include Caterpiller, Thermos and Walkman, while Xerox and Hoover have come dangerously close to losing their marks.

Audits

One way to avoid potential problems is to have an annual brand audit. Having regular audits will identify threats to your brand, and make sure it is being protected in your internal record keeping. As highlighted previously, if a mark has not been used for five years or longer it is vulnerable to attack for non-use. Third parties wanting to register or use the mark may be able to do so and have yours removed from the register. Keeping records of the use you're making of your trade mark, especially if it is nearing the five-year limit, is an invaluable way to help you protect your trade mark registration.

Having a system for keeping records of the countries in which the mark has been used – indicating when it was used, how it was used, and what marketing expenditure was involved – will be helpful for various reasons. For example, the onus of proof is on the trade mark owner to prove it has been using the mark if a third party challenges its use. It will be relatively easy to produce this proof if you've kept records of the mark's use.

On the other hand, if you're not intending to use the mark again, your records will make it easier to identify the mark in question – assuming that you have a number of marks – so you can ensure the mark is allowed to lapse and is not renewed.

Similarly, the audit should draw attention to any designs or domains coming up for renewal so you can decide whether or not to renew them. It should also aim to identify any further classes in which to extend the registration, and whether the marks are being used consistently. In addition, the audit should highlight whether further registrations are necessary in territories in which you may be selling your product.

Endangered trade marks

One situation where a trade mark could be at risk of losing its distinctiveness is where you coin a new word or term to describe an up-and-coming trend. If that word or term is not in general usage, you might be able to trade-mark it before the Trade Marks Registry realises that it is descriptive of the concept and therefore needs to be kept free for other traders to use.

Say, you have spotted the trend that social media was going to give rise to the need for a new service like 'reputation monitoring', and you secured the trade mark for the term 'reputation monitoring' before the trend was established. Would this be a coup? Well, you would be hard-pressed to stop competitors claiming that they also provide reputation monitoring services, and would be wasting your resources in trying to enforce such a non-distinctive trade mark.

Instead, it would be far better to have used your early understanding of an up-and-coming trend to make up a good suggestive term – such as Reputex. This would be a far more powerful trade mark than 'Reputation Monitoring' and would not be in danger of becoming generic.

There are only so many terms starting with the letters 'repu' that could be coined for this service, so by being early enough to invent a new name, you would be seizing the opportunity rather than wasting it by securing a descriptive trade mark.

As I've stressed throughout this book, it's important to get the right name if you want to end up with a mark that has intrinsic value.

Monitoring your IP

Monitoring your trade mark or other intellectual property is desirable so you can find out about potential infringements early on. It's easier to nip a potential problem in the bud before it has taken root.

The most basic monitoring would involve putting in place 'watch' services and Google Alerts, as discussed in Chapter 9. These services will give you advance notice of any applications or uses that infringe on your trade mark, domain name, patent, designs or copyright. As such, it puts you in a stronger position to prevent infringements or damage to your reputation and loss of revenue and even loss of a particular market.

If you are a substantial brand owner, you should put in place a system for monitoring auction sites such as eBay in order to detect infringements of your brand. By regularly conducting searches against your brand on Google, you can discover whether competitors are using your trade marks as metatags for their own websites, or on Google AdWords. This way you can keep an eye on how your trade mark is being used, to ensure the use does not cross the line of what the courts have deemed is acceptable (see Chapter 10).

Keeping tabs on your online presence, by checking for mentions of your name and other keywords, is an important way to protect and monitor your brand's reputation online. The reputation of a brand is much more likely to be damaged by competitors using similar names or passing themselves off as the brand, and potentially selling an inferior product or service that consumers wrongly believe to emanate from the brand itself.

Another way in which a brand's reputation can be damaged is through word of mouth. In Chapter 9, we looked at how social media has magnified the 'disgruntled customer' effect, and radically altered the dynamics of word of mouth.

A reputation may also be damaged through the actions of the business itself. The law recognises that companies work hard to build the goodwill and reputation associated with their products or services. So the law aims to protect consumers against mistakenly buying a product, thinking it is of a certain quality, only to find that it is from a different organisation and is designed to look like a recognised brand. If consumers don't realise it's a different organisation that is providing the product or service, the consumer suffers, as illustrated below.

Customer confusion

If you buy what you think is a Rolex but what you're actually getting is an expensive and poor-quality Ralax watch, clearly you have been misled into parting with your money for an inferior product. As a result, the Rolex brand's reputation could be adversely affected, even if the consumer later realised that the inferior watch did not emanate from Rolex. There is an expectation for Rolex to police the landscape and stop consumers being duped by lookalike or sound-alike products. That's why the law will help Rolex to stop its competitors from using similar names (such as Ralax) that could confuse consumers.

Trade mark law therefore prevents other traders from using the same or 'confusingly similar' names to sell products and services, and provides remedies for 'passing off' and trade mark infringement. (See Chapters 2, 5 and 9 for more information.)

However, as explained earlier, the law's protection cannot extend to descriptive names. Ownership rights in names are secured from trade marks, not from domain or company registration. So, it's important to have a name that may be registered as a word mark. You then know that the name on which you are building your brand can access the benefits of legal protection that the law affords in situations such as the Rolex and Ralax scenario example earlier.

With a monitoring service, you would be able to discover whether a third party is trying to register the same or a similar name as a trade mark. You could also watch the company and domain registers. It's much easier to do something about it before the other party secures a trade mark registration, or makes use of your mark, than it is to apply to cancel a registration that another party has secured. The longer someone has used a name, the more they will want to continue to use it. So disputes over their right to use a name can be difficult to negotiate to satisfactory conclusion.

A watch service provides regular searching of registers for applications made by third parties to register trade marks, patents, designs or domain names that may be similar or identical to yours. As we saw in Chapter 12, the trade mark system in the UK and in many other countries allows for any mark to be registered despite the existence of prior identical or similar registrations.

Also, third parties could obtain domain names that are almost identical to yours. Such a domain may be used to take advantage of the reputation built up in your website and cause confusion in the minds of your potential customers. (More about this in Chapter 16.)

Employees and Trading Standards

With the help of employees, distributors and licensees, you may be able to set up a news alert about any potential infringement. If you come across any infringements, take photographs of infringing goods on the market, make sample purchases and retain your receipts. Similarly, if you find evidence of copying or other incidents online, take screenshots to keep as evidence.

Trading standards officers are often under-resourced and overworked, but if you are able to enlist their help to enforce the Trade Descriptions Act and anti-counterfeiting provisions in the trade marks and copyright legislations, they might even be willing to bring criminal proceedings depending on the severity of the matter.

The officers have powers to make test purchases, and to enter and inspect premises and seize goods and documents. They can also obtain warrants to search premises if there are reasonable grounds to believe an offence is being committed. As a government body, Trading Standards is a more cost-effective option for enforcing your intellectual property rights as it bears the cost and takes action.

If the infringement involves counterfeiting and piracy, these are arrestable offences and you should report them to the police force.

Confusion logs

If you do discover third parties using names and marks similar to your marks, alert your employees, distributors and licensees and ask them to keep records of any evidence indicating that a likelihood of confusion has arisen.

Such confusion could include consumers mistakenly contacting you to complain about or to comment on the other product or how it is being advertised, or the media might ring you to ask you about the competing product, believing it to be yours. It could also be that stores mistakenly assume the product is yours and contact you for orders or queries about them.

In all situations of confusion, it helps to keep a note detailing the issues. This provides useful information about potential witnesses from whom you could take statements, should you decide to start infringement or passing off proceedings.

Conclusion

In this chapter, we looked at ways in which to protect your brand assets. As so much is now happening online, make sure you have a good understanding of copyright, social media, and infringing uses of your intellectual property, and monitor mentions of your brand online.

Chapter 13: Key take-home messages

■ Always use your trade mark in the exact form you have registered it, to avoid problems later when seeking to enforce your rights.

■ Be sure to register for trade marks in other countries as you expand your brand.

■ Remember to review your registration periodically in case you need to register in other classes.

■ Make sure you have regular audits to identify threats to your brand, and keep internal records of your own usage of it.

■ Beware of choosing a brand name that could easily become a descriptive or generic term.

■ Put in place 'watch' services and Google Alerts so you get advance notice of any infringements of your trade mark, domain name, patent, designs or copyright.

■ Take photographs or screenshots of incidents to keep as evidence.

■ Alert your employees, distributors and licensees to any third party usage of names and marks similar to yours, and ask them to keep records.

Chapter 14

Why a social media policy may be the best way to help your staff

'What used to be cigarette breaks could turn into "social media breaks" as long as there is a clear signal and IT isn't looking'
David Armano, Senior Vice President
at Edelman Digital

It's important for business owners who employ staff to consider their position on the issues presented by social media in order to draw up a policy, even if it's just a one-page document stating whether or not staff may have their own separate blogs. Such guidance will be helpful to staff, who may also want to know how they should refer to your business in their profiles.

For certain types of business, such as a professional services firm, it may be necessary to exercise extra care. Having in place a legal document that covers important policy issues is the best way to manage the risks.

One area of risk is copyright infringement, and it's vital for you and your staff to understand what images may and may not be used online, as discussed in previous chapters, including Chapter 6.

Terms of use and privacy policies of social media sites

A particular area of concern is the terms of use and privacy policies of the various social media sites. What are you signing up to when you agree to sign into a platform with your Twitter or Facebook ID? How should you best conduct yourself on the various platforms?

These are all issues for businesses to grasp and a good reason to train staff so that everyone is familiar with the basic information they need to know. This will include understanding how the technology works and how to engage on the various platforms. If you outsource social media to an external agency, you will need to be clear about what they will be doing and what you need to do. The best approach is one where you don't abdicate responsibility for engaging with your followers.

In this chapter, I will focus on why it's important to have a social media policy for staff and to keep it updated.

Why a social media policy is necessary

While this may seem more relevant to large businesses, in reality a social media policy is a good opportunity for any business, large or small, to think through its position on the variety of issues thrown up by social media. The objective should be to provide useful guidelines for staff.

Failure to seize the initiative means that problems and issues will surface that you have not considered, and this could have a damaging impact on your brand.

Any business employing staff typically needs to consider what policies it should put in place so that the business benefits from having well-connected staff and increased exposure but does not lose out if staff members leave.

If staff promote their own personal brand while they are in your employ, is it acceptable for them to take valuable contacts, possibly clients of yours, with them to their next job and use those contacts for the benefit of their new employer? If not, what would be a fair policy so they know in advance about what they may or may not do, and what your expectations will be if they leave your employment? Each business will have its own individual approach to such issues.

Before the advent of social media, if a member of staff arrived to work for you with their former employer's database and then proceeded to add it to your list, you would expect to have problems. However, social media makes it more difficult to know how to deal with similar issues, such as to whom contacts belong.

Given that on social media people want to do business with other people, it seems inevitable that you and your staff will engage on social media primarily by building personal brands. So, decide whether staff may have their own blogs rather than leaving it up in the air. Drawing up a policy is the ideal opportunity for considering such issues and taking advice on the pros and cons of a particular stance you may want to adopt. Employees need guidance, and employers should avoid the temptation to bury their heads in the sand. There must be appropriate training and clarity about roles.

The policy you adopt today may not be the one you will want to adopt for all time, but it's far better to start somewhere and then make changes as necessary than to create uncertainty within your business.

As soon as you have staff, implement a policy

As soon as your business employs staff, let them know about your brand values and your expectations of their behaviour when engaging on social media platforms. Even if you are the sole owner of a business, with no staff, your business will still have a culture and values, and it pays to consider what your policy should be. Then once you take on staff, or if you use outsourcers, you will be better placed to provide the necessary direction and clarity.

Your employment contracts should incorporate your company's social media policy and support your efforts to protect the business. Unfortunately, drafting legal documentation entails taking a negative mindset in order to focus on what might go wrong and to think through possible issues that could arise. However, this does make it less messy further down the line because airing expectations usually prevents problems.

The increasing trend for employees to develop their connections and increase their employability by engaging on social media means it's possible that they will arrive at your company with large Twitter and other social media followings, or even a popular industry blog.

The quality of the talent you retain, and having well-connected employees on social media, can bring your business increased exposure and extend its reach. Given that employees who develop a following online can have a beneficial impact on your business brand, it's not surprising that sometimes there's bad feeling when employees leave and take their connections with them. If there are any contacts that you would not want your staff to take with them when they leave your employment, this should be made clear in your social media policy.

Ownership of social media connections

There have been a few legal disputes over the ownership of social media connections when employees have left to work for a competitor.

In one case involving an employee who had developed a following on Twitter, and left the company with their following, a US company estimated the value of a Twitter follower at $2.50 per month – which is perhaps a little ambitious but it goes to show how seriously social media is increasingly taken by some businesses.

If you want to control the contacts that staff may take with them when they leave your company, it's more practical to focus on controlling specific connections. For example, if a member of staff is given a premium LinkedIn account, you may want to put in place some rules about what will happen to the connections they build up in that account during their employment with you.

One solution could be to take stock of their existing connections when they arrive at the company, and make it clear that certain – or all – connections that they make during their time in your employment are the property of your company, and that you require them to disconnect from those persons when they leave your employment and not to add them again within a certain time frame.

Followers of one person are unlikely to be interested in following their replacement and so may present little value to you. In this instance, transferring social media connections to yourself or a new employee is possibly inappropriate. It's more realistic and reasonable to simply specify what is off limits, for example copying names from your contact database and targeting your existing clients. There are no easy answers as, in practice, there can be serious and intractable problems for some businesses.

Database defence

In one case, the recruitment agency Hays brought legal action in 2008 after an employee allegedly appropriated a bunch of LinkedIn contacts. During the case, it was argued that Hays' database of contacts was the 'cornerstone' of the business.

In other cases, an employee's connections could be less critical to the business.

Why it's important to be clear about your values

A few examples from 2011 go some way towards illustrating why it is important to have clarity on the values and beliefs that your business subscribes to when staff begin to engage on social media. They also demonstrate how a social media policy can have a real impact.

Brand values

Apple had put in place a policy requiring employees' activity on social media to be consistent with its vision, and so when an employee poked fun at some Apple marketing and criticised his iPhone it was legitimate to dismiss him.

On the other hand, when Noah Kravitz left PhoneDog and took thousands of Twitter followers with him, his former employer did not have a clear policy to rely on, and found it necessary to bring legal action in an attempt to retrieve the account.

Reputation remedy

In the case, *Preece v. J D Wetherspoons*, an employee was dismissed after making negative comments about a pub's customers through Facebook. Her employer was subsequently successful at the Employment Tribunal because the company's social media policy provided for disciplinary action if comments on social media damaged its reputation.

Being clear about your values and beliefs makes it more possible to project a consistent image and attract like-minded employees.

An important aspect of branding is to communicate the ethos and values of the brand to employees so that your staff will be aligned to the values of the business. The amount of training which employees need in order to learn how to use social media platforms, what subjects are off limits, and how to avoid revealing confidential client information, depends on their age and job titles.

Conduct of staff

As well as impacting on the reputation of your business, the conduct of staff on social media can have implications on your legal liability.

For example, your business could be held liable if an employee was subjected to bullying by another member of staff via social media. Staff handbooks typically cover such issues as harassment and discrimination in the workplace, but it's important that these rules are now extended to cover interaction online.

Confidentiality is a serious issue for some businesses. If employees tweet about their work, there could be unintended breaches of confidential information, so it may make sense for businesses operating in sensitive areas like law or financial services to prohibit tweets about work matters.

Sometimes there are important subtleties to take into account. For example, if a member of staff mentions through social media that they are meeting a client, some sites, such as Foursquare, could automatically publicise information about the whereabouts of the meeting. If a number of employees are connected to an external contact through Facebook, there is a risk that an outsider could guess that they are a client of yours.

Piracy is rife online, but infringement of intellectual property can also happen accidentally. If your business is commissioned to produce copyright material, you may negotiate to give your clients the rights to the work. Therefore, your social media policy should alert employees not to publish online any details of work they are engaged on without authorisation as they would be infringing your client's rights.

Conclusion

As soon as you employ staff or use any outsourced help, you need to put in place a social media policy. In this chapter we looked at some of the factors to consider when developing a social media policy for your business. To some extent, the focus of the policy will depend on the industry in which you operate. There is no one-size-fits-all approach.

Once you've decided on your social media policy, it's appropriate to reflect the necessary elements within your employment and freelancer contracts.

Chapter 14: Key take-home messages

■ Drawing up a social media policy, and keeping it updated, is a good way for businesses to provide useful guidelines to staff on what to do and what not to do on social media platforms.

■ Communicate clearly the values and beliefs your business subscribes to so staff can be in synchrony with those values when engaging on social media.

■ The way your staff conduct themselves on social media not only impacts on your business's reputation but could also have implications on your legal liability.

■ Make sure that employment contracts and staff handbooks containing rules on harassment and discrimination in the workplace are extended to cover interaction online.

Chapter 15

Infringement of intellectual property: what's involved in litigation – and how to avoid it

'As a man is said to have a right to his property, he may be equally said to have a property in his rights' James Madison

In practice, many SMEs take risks that would not cost a lot to avoid. Understanding the risks that might arise will help you to build your business on solid legal foundations.

Common risks revolve around the use of names, designs and copyright material - particularly on websites - without sufficient legal due diligence.

Using others' IP materials without licence

Infringement can occur when you use someone else's copyright or designs without permission, or where you have permission but you use it in a way that goes beyond what was permitted.

Infringement also occurs where you make a product that incorporates a third party's IP and don't have a licence to do so. Another common pitfall is using a trade mark that is similar to someone else's, which could cause confusion.

However, it's not just your own actions that can cause you problems. If someone who works for you – such as your web designer – uses images for your site without an appropriate licence, then you are the one who is responsible as owner of the website.

Image problem

A client's web designer used several Getty images on her website. Several letters were sent to her from the solicitors acting for Getty, claiming sums running into several thousand pounds, despite the fact that she had had the images removed as soon as she received their letter. The designer, who was not based in the UK, refused to accept liability. It was only after we responded to the Getty solicitors that they stopped writing to her.

Even more common than copyright infringement is trade mark infringement. This type of infringement can have very serious repercussions for a business owner, due to the need to withdraw products from the market, change marketing materials and find a new identity.

Case study: Scrabulous

Two Indian brothers, Rajat and Jayant Agarwalla, created the game Scrabulous as a Facebook application in 2007.

The app allowed people to play a Scrabble-like game online – with friends, family, or anybody in the world – and quickly became very popular. The brothers thought it would be a smart idea to offer 'the world's favourite word game for free'.

As owner of the trade mark for Scrabble, Hasbro asked Facebook to shut Scrabulous down on the basis that it was infringing its trade mark. At the time of the incident, Scrabulous had thousands of players.

Had the creators of this game taken advice, they would have realised that trade mark law prevented them from using a similar name to Scrabble. Using Scrabulous traded off the goodwill of Scrabble, as it was the 'pulling power' of the name that got them the attention of consumers.

If they had used a name that did not infringe on a third party's trade mark rights, they would still be in business today. That is, assuming they could have become popular without associating themselves with the Scrabble trade mark.

Although Hasbro eventually created its own app, it is Zynga, the largest Facebook app creator, that has filled the gap left by Scrabulous, and it has done really well with its Words With Friends app.

App Store infringements

Trade mark infringement is a real risk with apps. Apps are available to an international audience, and many of the hundreds of new applications submitted to the App Store each day are unlikely to have had trade mark name checks. With hundreds of thousands of apps available for download at any one time, conflicts commonly arise. When rights collide, one of the developers needs to take the hit and rebrand, losing out on their investment in marketing, and suffering the costs of promoting a new name.

Some of the recent high profile cases include:

- **Starbucks, where an individual responsible for the iOS Starbucks Card Widget had to rename the app My Coffee Card.**

- **UberTwitter, an app for BlackBerry smartphones, was forced to rebrand after access to the Twitter API was revoked in part due to use of the Twitter trade mark.**

- **RIM, the company responsible for the BlackBerry, was caught off guard by a complaint from BASIS International over its use of the BBX name, eventually rebranding its latest software platform BlackBerry 10.**

The question of whether a trade mark is being 'used' by a third party in a way that infringes your trade mark rights can get quite technical sometimes. In every case, the first question is whether the infringing use is use as a trade mark or use as a badge of origin.

If it is not use as a trade mark (badge of origin), and is more general use, then it's unlikely to amount to trade mark infringement.

Passing off

To establish passing off you need evidence that you have goodwill in the unregistered sign – that is, in the name you are using. You also need to show that the other party's actions deceived your customers (which you'd do by taking statements from customers who were confused). If your case is strong, you might be able to get an injunction to prevent the other party from trading under the same name.

However, this is easier said than done. In practice, it's a complex and costly process that's likely to cost around £15,000 to £20,000, assuming that the matter doesn't need to go to full trial. Fighting a case in a full trial can result in a six-figure sum. Only the most well-resourced of companies could get justice in the courts if a full trial was needed.

One downside to not registering trade marks is that someone else in another part of the country may have been building up rights in a similar brand name without having registered it.

The solutions are generally unsatisfactory when two businesses are both using similar names. You often end up having to compromise and restrict your use of a name to a particular geographic area. Also, you won't then be able to register a trade mark. This is what happened with the popular 1990s boy band Blue.

Blue boy band

Blue started releasing singles quite unaware of the existence of another band named Blue in Scotland, which was a 70s rock band that had been using the name for longer. The original Blue wanted to stop the new Blue using the same name. They argued that their career and reputation was being damaged by the existence of the new Blue band. The matter settled on the basis that each band could continue to be known as Blue and trade under that name because the two bands were so different that it would be impossible to confuse the two. The judge in the case said that the bands could only continue using the same name as long as neither of them trade marked the name 'Blue'.

It's worth noting that if the original Blue had registered a trade mark, the new Blue would not have been allowed to continue using the name. A registered trade mark gives you better rights.

When new businesses are choosing names for their products and services, it's presumed that they will check the trade mark registers, which are public registers, just as a solicitor would search the Land Registry on behalf of a client who was buying a plot of land. Therefore, people are 'on notice' of names that are registered as trade marks. If someone else starts using the same name, they are automatically in the wrong. Failure to search is never an excuse.

Trade mark use and infringement

To establish that your trade mark has been used in an infringing way, it's necessary to show that a third party has, in the course of trade, used your mark, perhaps by affixing the mark to goods or packaging. The way that your mark has been used must fall into one or more of the following categories:

1. **It is identical to your registered trade mark and is used in relation to identical goods or services to those covered by your registration. So, for example, if your name is Interflora and your trade mark is registered to sell flowers, if someone else uses the name Interflora to sell flowers they would be using an identical mark in relation to identical goods.**

2. It is identical to your registered trade mark and is used in relation to goods or services similar to those covered by the registration. Here, what's being sold under the Interflora name is not flowers, but something similar that the public might think emanates from Interflora, such as a garden centre selling plants or Xmas trees. In such a scenario the complaint would be that the public may be confused into believing that Interflora was behind this other business as the goods are similar to those it sells.

3. It is similar to your registered trade mark in relation to goods or services that are identical to those covered by your registration. For example, if a business called itself Intrafleur and sold flowers, the public might be confused into thinking that the source of the flowers is Interflora.

4. It is similar to your registered trade mark in relation to goods or services similar to those covered by your registration (where the public is likely to be confused), for instance, if Intrafleur was a garden centre selling plants or Xmas trees.

5. It is identical or similar to your 'well-known' registered trade mark in relation to goods or services identical, similar or dissimilar to those covered by your registration. Here, the argument is that the use takes unfair advantage of, or is detrimental to, the distinctive character or repute of your 'well-known' mark.

As explained in Chapter 2, a well-known mark effectively has the same scope of protection as if the owner of the mark had registered in all 45 trade mark classes under the Nice Classification. In point 5, above, unfair advantage or detriment would be established by showing that the third party's mark will tarnish or dilute the distinctive character of your mark.

For example, if a recruitment agency set up and called itself Martini, the argument would be that the recruitment agency was using an identical name to the famous Martini trade mark, albeit in relation to a dissimilar service. Therefore, the use would be infringing Martini's trade mark rights by taking unfair advantage of its well-known name.

Rebranding

As we saw with the Scrabulous example earlier, you risk having to rebrand (and pay damages) if the reason you cannot own a name is that someone else has better rights to it. This is not a risk worth taking, given that it is relatively inexpensive to check the name that you intend to use.

The time to consult a brand lawyer is early on, before you've invested too much in the name. As the trade mark registers are cluttered with names, it's never a good idea to be too attached to a particular name. It makes sense to have a shortlist of names available.

If you are required to rebrand, generally you will have to find a new name and create new marketing materials at short notice. Products will have to be recalled from the market. So, trade mark infringement is something to be wary off, particularly if you would have to recall and repackage goods. This could prove extremely costly.

As mentioned previously, a trade mark infringement action could surface at any time, even years after you've established your brand and are reliant on the income of the business.

These are the reasons for making sure the name you've picked is sound. If you suspect you have a problem with the name you're using, rebrand in your own time without waiting for the trade mark owner to object to your use of the mark.

If you are using a name you cannot own, the more successful your business becomes, the more likely you are to come to the attention of the existing trade mark owner. Therefore, in many ways the best thing that could happen to you would be if the trade mark owner finds out about you early on in the life of your business, so you can rebrand and enjoy success with a name you can own.

What rebranding entails when you infringe on others' trade marks

It's important to take on board what is actually entailed when you are forced to rebrand. You don't generally have the option to simply redirect your old domain name to your new one. You may even be required to hand over your customer lists.

The rationale behind the law is that it was the name, and its associations in the public's mind that drew customers to use your product or service in the first place, so those customers really belong to the brand owner and not to you.

That is why the owners of Scrabulous couldn't simply choose a new name and then alert all their users that Scrabulous now has a new name. In effect, they had to vanish and start over from scratch.

However, if you find that someone is infringing on your trade mark, a reason to tread carefully is the 'unjustified threats' provisions in legislation.

Unjustified threats

If someone else is using your trade mark, design or patent, in an infringing way, make sure you consult a lawyer rather than approaching the business owner directly. The 'unjustified threats' rule is a concept that was introduced to protect innocent manufacturers who tend to react fearfully and to the detriment of their business interests if accused of infringement.

The possibility of litigation is enough to dissuade them from what they are doing, even if they have a strong case. If you fall foul of the unjustified threats rule, it could put you in the wrong, and expose you to litigation by the other party.

Some people argue that there is no need for such rules to protect the innocent and that all it achieves is to force rights-owners to sue first, without having the sort of preliminary correspondence which in the majority of cases resolves a matter, at much less cost to all concerned.

Nevertheless, the legislation exists, and makes it necessary to be careful how you deal with infringements of your trade mark, design or patent rights.

The test of what is a threat is very broad and any hint at bringing proceedings could be deemed to be a threat.

If you send a 'cease and desist' letter (see below) and it is deemed to be unjustifiable, the person receiving the threat will be able to sue you for damages. So, always get legal advice before using the threat of legal proceedings.

Copyright

Although copyright is not currently subject to the 'unjustified threats' rule, a proposal was put forward in the Digital Economy Act 2010 to introduce such provisions.

To recap, the unjustified threats rule means you risk being sued if you threaten third parties with trade mark, patent or design infringement proceedings. Therefore, take great care over how you handle infringement situations.

Cease and desist letters

When the potential damage to reputation is caused by someone else using a mark that others may mistake as emanating from you, the first step usually involves sending a 'cease and desist' letter to the person responsible. Cease and desist letters are used for other types of intellectual property infringement too, not just trade marks.

The English courts expect owners of intellectual property assets to follow a reasonable and proportionate procedure before taking legal action against an infringer. The letter to the infringer would detail your claim by outlining the rights you own, and your complaint, so that the other party understands it and can investigate the claim.

The letter should enclose copies of the essential documents you are relying on, such as your trade mark or design certificate, and any evidence of the infringement. It is normal to give a period of time in which to respond, although this does depend on what rights have been infringed and how.

For blatant infringements, a strongly worded cease and desist letter aimed at securing an undertaking to stop the infringing activities would be appropriate.

In really urgent cases, you might not have time for a cease and desist letter and may have to rush off and apply for an injunction without delay and without even notifying the infringer. However, this only applies in exceptional situations. Normally a letter would be the appropriate way to avoid jeopardising your position.

Interim injunction

One of the remedies available for an infringement is an interim injunction. This is an order of the court, either compelling the other party to do something or prohibiting them from doing something. For example, an injunction could require your competitor to stop selling products bearing a sign that resembles your trade mark.

Generally, in infringement situations an interim injunction is sought as a temporary and urgent remedy which lasts until the matter comes to trial. A permanent injunction might then be granted at the trial, after the court has heard the case and reached a decision on the merits.

As an injunction is an order of the court preventing any further infringement, breaking the terms of an injunction is a contempt of court, which can lead to imprisonment. In practice, few cease and desist letters result in an application for an interim injunction, because the letter effectively achieves a resolution of the dispute. The fear of engaging in court proceedings is usually sufficient incentive for the parties to compromise and settle.

There may be a lot of posturing before settlement, and offers to settle may specify a lower amount than the sum you claimed or that the other side is actually willing to pay. That's just the way negotiations tend to go, and you never know whether the other party is serious or just bluffing, so you risk losing the chance of a settlement each time you reject their offer.

Some correspondence will ensue before a final compromise is reached or the matter is escalated to the stage where legal proceedings are issued. So it can be quite unpleasant to be involved in a dispute. However, in many situations, especially where small businesses are involved, after some correspondence back and forth the matter is generally resolved.

Where matters do reach court for an interim injunction or a declaration, it is rare that they go on to full trial unless the parties are well resourced or there is a lot at stake. The potential exposure to costs jumps to the £100,000-plus mark if a matter is allowed to proceed to full trial.

The courts encourage the parties to try to reach a compromise, and require you to have attempted alternative dispute resolution, or ADR as it's known in short, before trial.

ADR

ADR is a type of dispute resolution where there is no third party judge deciding the outcome. It is quite unlike traditional court proceedings and its other alternatives such as expert determination, or arbitration.

ADR aims to help the parties to reach a mutually satisfactory agreement. A third party facilitates the outcome, but does not decide what that outcome should be.

The rationale behind ADR is that focusing on the rights and wrongs of the situation escalates many disputes and results in the parties maintaining entrenched positions, thus preventing compromise and resolution of the case.

ADR tends to have a higher chance of successfully resolving a dispute where there is a relationship that needs to be preserved because it gives the parties an incentive to reach a compromise.

If ADR fails to achieve settlement the next step would be legal proceedings.

Legal proceedings

The uncertainties inherent in litigation and the prohibitive expense involved mean that only a tiny number of disputes end up being argued in court. The parties have a real incentive to reach agreement rather than risk losing the case and having to pay the other side's costs. However, although the successful party may get costs awarded against the other side, they will not recover all their own costs, and will typically be out of pocket by as much as one third of the overall costs.

Where the dispute needs to be taken to court, it will usually be dealt with by the Patents Court initially. Your lawyers set out the full details of your complaint in a document known as particulars of claim. The other party then serves its defence. If the matter does not settle, there will be a case management conference at the court when the court gives directions on the future conduct of the case.

The next major milestone is known as 'disclosure', which is when both sides have to exchange the documentary evidence that their case is relying on, such as written statements of witnesses and any expert reports. Most cases settle at this stage, as it's easier to see the strength and weaknesses in the case when you know what evidence the other side has to support their case at trial.

All this will have taken 18 months or so and if the case goes to trial, the losing party faces the possibility of having to pay its own legal costs as well as those of the other party.

The name determines costs of enforcement

Earlier in this book I mentioned that some names are more expensive to enforce than others. If you are aware of this when you're choosing a name for your business, you are better placed to make an informed choice. While some of the best names are suggestive ones, made-up names have more potential to give you a clear territory to call your own. For this reason, proper names will require less money to protect than names incorporating common words. So, a name like Ryanair would be cheaper to protect than easyJet.

However, it takes more time, money and resources to promote made-up names, or proper names like Ryanair. This is why marketers prefer to use names that describe or suggest the business activity, such as easyJet.

In domain disputes, third parties who have registered similar domain names to your brand name would find it more difficult to justify their actions if they have used a proper or made-up name. They would have to give plausible reasons why using a name similar to your brand name was legitimate rather than in 'bad faith'. It's far easier therefore to recover domain or company names incorporating your brand name from third parties if you have a distinctive, made-up name.

The brand represents a significant proportion of marketing spend and if things go wrong, it will represent a significant proportion of your legal budget to enforce your rights.

Other intellectual property infringement

Apart from your trade mark, you will have other intellectual property such as copyrights, know-how, designs or even a patent, which could potentially be infringed. The principles are much the same as for trade mark infringement in terms of unjustified threats (except for copyright infringement where the concept does not apply). Copyright infringement is discussed in more detail in Chapter 7, but, as with litigation in general, if a letter of claim to the other party does not resolve the dispute the next step tends to be court proceedings.

Remember, a popular misconception when it comes to copyright is that if you acknowledge the author then it's not infringement. However, acknowledging or crediting someone as the author is not enough. You need their permission or you must be able to successfully establish that it's 'fair dealing'.

Defences to copyright and design infringement

The defences to copyright infringement are broadly that the use was fair dealing – that is, it was for the purposes of private study or research for non-commercial purposes, or that it was for the purpose of criticism or review and news reporting.

For UK registered designs, it is an infringement to make, offer, put on the market, import, export, use, or stock any product that either incorporates your design or to which your design is applied. The infringing use does not necessarily involve copying your design.

A successful defence to design infringement would be that the design created a different overall impression to the copied design in the eyes of an informed user (that is, a person who is familiar with the particular sector to which the design applies).

There are certain other defences too, such as private, non-commercial use; use for teaching purposes; or use in a component part used for the repair of a complex product in order to restore its original appearance.

To prevent a third party arguing that they were an innocent infringer and were unaware that your design was registered, you should ensure that any product incorporating your design or to which your design is applied is clearly marked with the word 'registered design' and accompanied by the registered number of the design.

Visual identity, trade dress, and passing off

Trade dress, or 'get-up', refers to the features of the visual appearance of a product or its packaging, or the appearance of shops or their decor. These represent ways in which a business may be recognised by its customers.

The individual features, or appearance, include the size, shape and colour schemes of a product as well as distinctive packaging or the arrangement of labels.

Accordingly, 'get-up' is often relied on during passing off proceedings in addition to the name or mark. For example, the packaging and name of the well-known 'Penguin' biscuits were held to be distinctive features of Penguin biscuits, which 'Puffin' biscuits had copied.

Jif Lemon lookalike

A case that became the hallmark of protection of the get-up for goods was that of Jif in 1990. The House of Lords decided that the lemon-shaped, yellow plastic bottle used by the business over many years as a container for its lemon juice was so distinctive that shoppers would disregard the fact that the lemon juice contained in a competitor's similar container bore a completely different label and name. In other words, members of the public would rely on the lemon-shaped container in making their purchases, believing that such a container indicated that the product emanated from Jif.

Where the get-up or packaging of a product has become sufficiently distinctive, it can be protected. This is an area in which a combination of features may become capable of being protected by the law of passing off, even where there may be difficulties in obtaining trade mark protection under trade mark law.

So if you've arrived at a unique differentiating proposition – a distinctive way of offering your products or services or packaging them – you may be able to resort to the law to stop a competitor copying your winning formula, depending on the particular circumstances. For example, if a business has established a very distinctive decor, consisting of a combination of features, such as a Starbucks interior, it would be possible to take an action in passing off to protect the get-up of the premises if a competitor copied them too closely. Often in cases that arise, a competitor will have cynically copied various elements of the get-up and sometimes even chosen a similar name too.

The law of passing off protects the goodwill and reputation of a business against unfair exploitation by others.

Conclusion

In this chapter, we looked at some of the consequences that could follow if you infringed on third parties' rights, or if someone else has infringed your rights. The important thing is not to resort to self-help if someone has infringed your trade mark, design or patent, as you do not want to run the risk of receiving a claim for unjustified threats.

Chapter 15: Key take-home messages

■ Trade mark infringement can have serious repercussions for a business and can be costly if goods have to be recalled and repackaged.

■ Tread carefully when dealing with infringements of your trade mark, design or patent rights, to avoid falling foul of the 'unjustified threats' rule.

■ Even if you think you have a good case, it's best to settle disputes without going to court to avoid costly litigation fees.

■ Be aware that if a case were to end up in court, you wouldn't recover all your costs, even if you won the case.

■ It's easier and cheaper to protect a distinctive, made-up name or a proper name than a descriptive one.

Chapter 16

Domain registration and disputes: how to beat the cybersquatters and retrieve domains in disputes

'A long dispute means both parties are wrong'
Voltaire

If you want to check the availability of a domain name, then use a reputable site or, better still, use your browser. There is anecdotal evidence that some disreputable services abuse information they collect from searches conducted on their registers by registering names searched, for domain tasting. One approach involves buying the domain name to see if it is lucrative and, if it's not, returning it at the end of the free taster period. So, unless you are ready to buy the domain straight away, it's safest to search for available domains via your browser.

Rights in domain names are established in a contract between registrant and registrar. Therefore, register domains in your own name, using your own email address. If you delegate the task to a website designer or an employee, ask them not to register the domain in their name, using their own email address, as this could lead to problems.

For example, if an employee left your employ, and the renewal notice went to an email address no longer in use, you could lose the domain and, with it, your website. Web designers have been known to register domains in their own name, move to another country, and claim the site as their own. Alternatively, they might refuse to let the site owner engage another designer to implement new functionality needed by the site.

Even if you trust your designer, it's not a good idea to have them register your domain in their own name. What if they were to fall ill and go into hospital and miss the domain renewal reminder? Losing the domain would mean losing your site and, if they have not backed up the website, which some web designers fail to do, you would not be able to simply restore the site. You would lose all your content, images – everything.

Domaining

The domain name system works on a first-come, first-served basis, and some domain name speculators who got there first profited significantly. The practice of domaining involves creating a large domain name portfolio by registering many domain names to earn income through advertising. Top domainers can earn profits running into millions of pounds from the registration of hundreds of thousands of domain names. Often there is a premium value on generic domain names like books, sex, wine, pets, and so on, so that such domain names change hands for millions of dollars.

One downside for the prospective Internet business owner is that many domain names have already been registered by other parties.

Check the trade mark registers before registering domains

The price of the domain you want to purchase could be substantial, so it's advisable not to approach others with a view to purchasing a domain name until you've established that the domain name is available to register as a trade mark.

When your chosen domain name is registered, but is not being used for any business activity, it may be 'parked' and used for 'click farming' – this is the practice of using the domain to attract traffic and generate click revenue.

Earning from Google or other search engines

Earning revenue from click farming involves being paid a commission by Google or other search engine each time an advertiser's ad is clicked on at the domain in question. Although the amounts paid per click may be quite low, the numbers can soon mount up to large figures for a high-volume site.

The revenue comes from Google or other search engines, because these are the search engines that feature their advertisers' pay per click ads.

Cybersquatting

Cybersquatting is to be distinguished from the business of domaining. Cybersquatters use domains for click farming, but the main difference between them and domainers is that cybersquatters do not have legitimate claims to the name. Very often they will email a company telling it that they have a domain name that the company would want and that they will only transfer that name for a large sum of money.

In this situation, it's important to avoid responding with angry emails. If the domain is not too important to you, consider waiting for a while. Once the cybersquatter realises that the domain is not valuable to you, and if the website at the domain doesn't get many hits, the cybersquatter will probably not renew it.

If you decide to wait it out, register the domain for a snapback service which will automatically purchase the domain name for you when it becomes available.

Using a fake email address

In order to avoid legal costs, many companies who discover that someone owns a domain name they want, register a fake email account and approach the domain name owner, asking to buy the domain name for a small fee. In many instances, the domain name can be purchased for less than the cost of launching a legal complaint. If trying this approach, be careful not to reveal who you are at any time or tell them what you need the domain name for.

This technique is also best saved for a website that you will not actually use and simply want to prevent someone else from setting up with that name; you do not want the cybersquatter to realise you are paying out for websites as it only encourages them to engage in more of this behaviour, and soon afterwards they are likely to register a bunch of domain names similar to your trade mark.

If you successfully acquire a domain name in this way, it's best to use a third party as the registrar or to use a privacy service. You should probably also use an escrow service for transfer of the money, as there have been several cases where money was paid but the domain was never transferred. (An escrow service is a licensed and regulated company that will collect and hold your money and only send it on to the seller once the domain has been transferred to you.)

However, cybersquatters are increasingly aware of this technique, and realise that domain buyers are not necessarily who they say they are, or if they are, that they are buying on behalf of another entity. If you are dealing with a knowledgeable domain owner, expect them to be very cautious. They will want to know as much about the potential buyer as possible in order to either maximise the sale or to prevent a UDRP (Uniform Domain-Name Dispute-Resolution Policy issue, discussed below) action against them later.

Companies are known to use the domainer's willingness to sell as evidence of bad faith in a UDRP simply because the owner names a price that he would sell at.

Domain disputes

If you discover that someone else has a domain name with your company or product name on it, you must decide whether to use the court system by filing a suit in court or whether to initiate the dispute-resolution procedure available for the particular domain suffix.

Two of the benefits of arbitration over litigation are that it is generally cheaper and faster. The fees for filing a dispute-resolution claim are lower and you will not need to go to the expense of having a trial.

Each type of domain suffix has its own registration body and dispute-resolution procedures. The Uniform Domain-Name Dispute-Resolution Policy – which for .co.uk domains is Nominet – allows the person claiming rights in a name to apply for domains registered in 'bad faith' to be transferred or cancelled.

To win in this type of arbitration you will need to prove three elements, namely that:

■ **you have prior rights in the name;**

■ **the owner does not have rights in the name; and**

■ **The domain name was registered and is being used in bad faith.**

Satisfying these three criteria is not straightforward, and their application and interpretation can vary according to the particular individual or panel assigned to decide your case, but in some situations the process can offer a useful cost-effective remedy.

The main limitation of the UDRP is that if you are successful, you only will be awarded transfer of the domain name. The tribunal does not have the power to award any money, so you will not get any damages or legal costs.

However, transfer of the domain may be all you can realistically achieve. This is especially true in cases where the registrant is based in a jurisdiction that is out of your reach for enforcement of court orders or is using a cloaked identity. Service of legal notice under domain name arbitration requires only proof that you tried to contact the registrant using the available information (which will be the details you can glean by doing a 'whois' search to find out who owns the domain name).

Confiscation of domain names

In one case, an entrepreneur had started up his own business spending £100,000 on a website and on search engine optimisation. However, he then faced confiscation of his domain names because they were too similar to the market leader's brand name in his industry. He had not taken any legal advice, and was under the misapprehension that he could use the domain name. The fact that the domain name was very similar to a registered trade mark in another country, had escaped him as being a cause for concern.

He was astonished to find one day that all his top-level domain names had vanished from his portal. The domains had been taken because the trade mark owner had initiated an action to recover them. Not only had the business owner used domain names similar to the other company's trade mark, but he had also copied many of its copyright materials, such as its terms of business.

Getting ready for action

To initiate an action, start by collecting evidence. Are there references on the website to you or to your competitors? Check the whois facility to find out who owns the domain name. There are disreputable whois sites so be sure to use the whois service of a reputable site like domaintools.com

When you do a whois search, don't be surprised if the domain is registered to a fictitious name or if the registrant is using a name shield, as discussed below. Check the date when the domain was registered to the current owner. If they registered the domain name before you began your business, the case is much more difficult to prove and your options for recourse are more limited.

Name shield

A name shield means that the registrant's name is displayed as 'Whois Guard' (a system that protects the privacy of a website owner). This will make it more difficult to determine the identity of the real registrant, but it will not prevent you from getting transfer of the domain names either in court or through arbitration.

If the name is not shielded, find out whether there have been previous UDRP proceedings against the owner. Evidence of their having lost previous arbitration proceedings will be useful in your own case since it is evidence of bad faith. Some country-level domains (such as .uk) even have special rules for registrants who have had several decisions made against them, and in such cases the cybersquatter will have a much higher burden of proof in preventing the transfer of the domain.

Ask your lawyers to write to the owner to state your claims and demand transfer of the domain. If the registrant of the domain is a legitimate domainer, they are more likely to agree to settle with you for fear of being labelled a cybersquatter in a judgment. When dealing with cybersquatters the rule of thumb is to be prepared for almost anything.

Cyberflight

One common practice, known as cyberflight, is where the registrant, soon after being contacted, quickly transfers the domain to another party or another name. If this happens before you have filed your dispute-resolution claim or lawsuit, then you will generally have to serve another letter on the new registrant unless there is good evidence that it is the same registrant.

You can usually tell this by assessing whether the website has changed and whether there have been other changes, such as the website's server.

Once you file suit in a dispute-resolution procedure or in court, the domain is locked. However, cyberflight can occur during the time lapse between your filing suit and the domain name being locked. If it occurs during this period, you will probably be able to amend the complaint rather than having to start from scratch, because courts or tribunals tend to regard the complaint as having the same registrant.

Dispute-resolution bodies

The criteria for the Uniform Domain-Name Dispute-Resolution Policy, the policy applicable to .com, .net, .org and other top-level domains, generally require you to establish that the domain that's been registered by a third party is identical or confusingly similar to your brand name.

One of the benefits of litigation over UDRP is that there a large number of remedies available, including damages. It's also possible to get an undertaking from the squatter not to register any names in the future that infringe against your trade mark rights. Additionally, cybersquatters often have to pay damages and legal fees in addition to transferring the domains.

Benefit of trade mark registration

To be successful in an UDRP dispute, it helps to have a trade mark registration. This can make short work of the requirement to demonstrate rights in the name. Otherwise, you will need to establish that you have goodwill in the name, along the same lines as it is necessary to establish in passing off cases, as we saw in Chapter 15.

It's generally more straightforward to prove bad faith if the brand name is distinctive, such as when it is a proper name like Microsoft.

Microsoft litigation

A few years ago Microsoft had a very effective campaign against typosquatters who had registered common misspellings of its name and were deriving click revenue from Google each time people searched using the misspellings.

Cybersquatting was becoming a serious problem for Microsoft, so it launched legal actions against a number of cybersquatters in the United States and the United Kingdom. It publicly denounced the typosquatters who had registered slight variants of its brand and had been earning money from adverts they placed on the pages that people mistakenly visited.

In the United States, Microsoft filed six lawsuits against typosquatters and settled with an untold number of them. One of these lawsuits was to reveal the identities of 54 domain name owners. In the end, it was able to recover thousands of domain names and damages. In one case in California, Microsoft was awarded $1 million in damages in a case against a cybersquatter who had registered 85 infringing domain names. Microsoft was also successful in the United Kingdom where it launched five legal actions that allowed it to recover over 6,000 domain names.

It hopes to take further action in other countries against other cybersquatters. Aaron Kornblum, senior attorney for Microsoft, said: 'We hope that our stance and activity on this issue will help motivate and empower other companies whose brands are abused to take action'.

The domain owners were infringing Microsoft's trade mark by sending traffic intended for Microsoft to other sites or to web pages collecting click revenue by featuring links of computer-related businesses advertising on Google's AdWords system.

Descriptive domains

If the domain name you are using for your brand is purely descriptive, there is little you can do to stop others using a similar domain name. So, if you do intend to use a descriptive domain name, consider combining it with your brand name.

For example, at Azrights we use azrightstrademarkregistration.co.uk. This is a little unwieldy, but at least if we begin to rank for the term 'trade mark registration', and searchers go back to find us, they are unlikely to get confused by similar domain names. Including our brand name as a prefix makes it less likely that our potential customers would go to the wrong site when looking to find our site again.

If we just used trademarkregistration.co.uk, then there is nothing to stop competitors securing trade mark registration using other suffixes and it's far more likely that traffic that was looking for us would end up going to the wrong site.

Although in theory you might claim passing off when others register similar descriptive domain names, it would be an uphill battle to persuade a judge that others should be stopped from using a similarly descriptive name that is not capable of being trade-marked by you – for example, a name like Hotels.com.

Conclusion

This chapter has shown how the domain registration system interacts with trade marks to provide powerful rights to brands with a distinctive brand name like Microsoft. If you have a name like Apple, or Shell, it's easier for domainers to put forward arguments to persuade the authorities that they did not register the corresponding domain name in bad faith.

Chapter 16: Key take-home messages

■ When checking the availability of a domain name, always use a reputable site or your browser.

■ Always register domains in your own name, using your own email address.

■ Check the trade mark registers before registering domains.

■ If you want to prevent someone from using your domain name, arbitration is usually cheaper and faster than litigation.

■ With a descriptive domain name, there's little you can do to stop others using a similar name, so consider combining it with your brand name.

■ The rule of thumb when dealing with cybersquatters is to be prepared for almost anything.

Conclusion

Clearly, IP is relevant to every business, not just to those traditionally considered to be in IP rich industries.

As IP law is a complex subject, most people reading this book still need help to identify how IP issues and intangibles impact their business. Nowadays, much of the value any business generates is attributable to intangibles, such as your knowledge, relationships, reputation, content, innovations, websites, brand and more. Ultimately, it's such intangibles that enable you to make profits. Some intangibles are protectable as intellectual property assets while others, though not IP, could be as significant and hence, need to be carefully managed.

To build a business in which you generate and own important IP assets, and avoid infringing on the rights of others it's important to be able to identify the different intangibles that exist. While you may not necessarily want to set aside a budget to prioritise acquiring every possible IP asset, understanding the risks and opportunities helps you to secure assets and avoid wasting money on IP protection which may be inappropriate at a particular point in time. For example, many businesses at start up stage could use a temporary or descriptive name so as to avoid the need to spend on trade mark registration. Many world famous brands started out with a different name to the one they are known by today, so avoiding the high expenditure on domain names and trade mark registration could make sense when a business concept is still not proven.

Sometimes companies focus on one type of intangible, such as a patent, and leave themselves without funds for any other IP rights. This could seriously expose the business, and result in neglect of IP that may be more valuable to the business. The fact that you can protect something with a patent does not necessarily mean it's a good investment, although this is not to say that prioritising a patent application over everything else is always inappropriate. It depends what you're getting in the way of protection. If it will give you a strong patent, and competitive advantage then it's absolutely essential. Otherwise, it may be misguided use of limited resources.

A point to bear in mind is that a patent attorney who hopes to register your patent in return for offering free advice may not necessarily be the right person to look to for independent commercial guidance on whether or not a patent application would be a good idea. That is why there is a need for independent commercial advice to help a business to determine how to prioritise and exploit intangibles. Businesses, even those in the same industry are likely to reach different conclusions about how best to budget for and prioritise their IP needs. Each business has a different plan, its own agenda, and objectives, and so will have its own unique legal requirements. So your IP strategy as a business should reflect your circumstances, long-term goals and aspirations.

What help is available to companies?

Although there is a general focus in society (in the UK at least) on raising awareness about IP, there is currently little in the way of services available to help ordinary small businesses to identify, understand and manage their intangibles. Instead, advice and information tends to be thrown in incidentally as part of assessing whether a business has a need for various IP services. However, as the context in which such advice is offered is to identify services for a business to buy, there is little scope to focus on strategic decision taking on IP needs.

Traditionally, IP audits have been the way companies have discovered what IP they have and what steps they need to take to better protect their IP. However, inevitably with an IP audit you're left with a long list of services to buy and little real opportunity to discover the pros and cons of the different IP rights, nor how to best prioritise your scarce resources. Even if you then proceed to register your IP and put in place legal contracts, what do you do then? If you launch a new brand, hire a new recruit, develop a new product or enter another foreign market how do you know what to do to protect your position without having to spend yet another set of fees on legal advice? And if you don't spend, then how do you avoid getting into a mess with your IP?

Long term, you need more than a handful of registration certificates. What's needed is a way to work out how to prioritise resources, and know what to look out for to manage independently.

That's why we developed the IP Wizard service. It offers guidance so businesses can reach strategic decisions on how best to manage their IP, and make informed decisions about which matters to defer, and which to address immediately.

A service giving a business the space to question whether or not to proceed with particular IP services is particularly appropriate if you are intending to sell the business in the future. It would be appropriate to find out about gaps in your IP ownership, or contractual position, and plan how to address any deficiencies in a timescale to suit your budget and available time. Like that you don't risk seeing the sale price on your business drop should your buyer's due diligence team discover deficiencies.

There are a number of ways in which IP issues arise as part of the day to day decisions companies may be involved with. Clearly, it's not sustainable to seek legal advice every time a transaction is to be entered into by the business, so how can companies avoid the pitfalls so their people are equipped to recognise and flag up matters with IP implications and know what initial documentation to use to protect the company's interests?

The IP Wizard helps businesses to understand IP risks and opportunities, to use first aid tools, and to know when to seek legal advice.

Some of the issues which can impact your IP position day to day, influence the value of your business, and affect your exposure to risk include:

- **Terms of client engagement.** The basis on which you take on new clients or sell to customers determines your relationships and helps manage expectations. These terms are rarely a one-off document that is prepared and forgotten. They should be constantly reviewed and updated as a business grows and develops, and introduces new products or services.

- **Brands and trade marks.** A name must be legally effective and available for your purposes otherwise it cannot be perfect for you. Leaving out the legal dimension when choosing a name is equivalent to building on a plot of land you don't own. Just as with land, it's possible to do a number of checks so with names, you should get an opinion on whether a name is legally sound. Names have the potential to contain the value of your business, if you succeed. Also, worth considering is how expensive it would be to enforce your rights in a name. So the job's only half done when you find a name to which your target market responds.

- **Competitors** commonly copy a successful business by using similar names and logos to divert business to themselves. Having a good name, which is legally protected through trade mark registration, is the best defence. So, a name protects your business as well as being your brand identity. If there is a need to change names, the time to rebrand and get a distinctive name for your business is in the early years. It's too disruptive later.

- **Your innovations.** Don't exaggerate the significance of patents. The reality is that a patent will sometimes give powerful protection against competition, and sometimes not. Patents are costly to secure, and bring with them the disadvantage of having to disclose your ideas to the world. Whether it's worth applying for a patent depends on your invention, and a host of other issues. So, a discussion about the pros and cons of patenting with someone who is able to offer commercial advice that takes account of the power of other IP, such as copyright and trade marks is the ideal starting point.

- **Databases.** Keep track of contact details on your database so you have good information and know how you met someone, and what their area of expertise is. Often the database can acquire a significant value, particularly if you decide to sell the business later. So, to make it more likely that it will pass due diligence tests when lawyers are handling your business sale keep a record of each person's consent to receive your emails, and update your list by removing inactive contacts after a period.

- **There are a host of other legal issues.** Your profile, and online branding, SEO and internet marketing are examples of other critically important IP. There are a number of issues concerning your website to consider, and these will matter unless your website plays a very minor part in your business. Assess the risks on social media and pay attention to employment arrangements as they significantly impact on IP ownership.

The IP Wizard provides a road map to know how to deal with IP matters as a business starts up, grows and develops. It's also the ideal way to introduce systems and procedures in your business so your team can flag up IP issues that arise day to day.

As an entrepreneur, I'm naturally keen to solve problems when I notice that a market need is not well met. That is how the IP Wizard service was born. It's a disruptive solution in the sense that unlike traditional IP audits the result isn't a laundry list of legal issues aimed at bringing more work into the firm. Instead, it genuinely helps clients be more intelligent in the way they set about protecting their IP position and use lawyers. They have space to reach sound commercial decisions about the legal work they may need.

Branding agencies

A separate problem in need of a solution is the widespread lack of knowledge about how IP is relevant to branding or websites. Many small design agencies are keen to get access to IP assistance, as they worry they may pick a name for a client, or develop a logo which will be infringing. They realise it would reflect poorly on them to get it wrong, but on the other hand, the complexity of IP laws is a real hurdle. This leads some designers to curb their creativity. For example, one agency told me they opt for names by looking to see if the dot com is available, on the basis that such a name is unlikely to infringe on third party rights. Other designers say they avoid creating logo images due to the risk of infringement.

I would love to hear from design agencies, or their clients to find out more about their experiences with IP law. Do, please get in touch through my personal website; http://www.shireensmith.com/contact/

The single most important point to take on board from reading this book is that IP law is relevant when you create a brand. It's not just for protecting something already created. For example, names must be legally available and effective before any design work is undertaken. Many choices of brand element involve IP considerations, such as whether it is distinctive enough to protect, and whether a particular protection strategy will give you a competitive advantage. So, IP is not something to leave till your branding is completed. By then you may have far less valuable IP to protect.

Once you have something distinctive, protect it properly so you don't lose its value, and can prevent copying. Just remember the Coca-Cola bottle. Had it not been protected with a design registration it would have been impossible for Coca-Cola to go on to secure the monopoly right it now enjoys over this iconic bottle shape.

Last Words

As a society, we're good at knowing how to deal with the physical things, the tangibles, but when it comes to intangibles, we're less sophisticated. As digitisation disrupts every industry, and technology issues become relevant to every business, intellectual property law is increasingly playing a central role in business. Intangibles are often the most valuable assets companies generate, yet few SMEs have a way to distinguish between the different types of intangibles, and to know which of them constitutes IP that the law will protect. Nor do the majority of businesses know enough about IP law, to appreciate what steps to take to protect their intangible assets beyond perhaps registering a trade mark. Every business in the information economy needs to seek guidance on how to manage its intangibles.

Reaching decisions which pay early attention to IP is the best way to serve the aspirations of businesses, increase the value they generates, and bring long term prosperity.

With publications like this book, or the introduction of new offerings like the IP Wizard, I hope to equip entrepreneurs, and business owners with the tools they need to face the challenges of the knowledge economy.

Remember that your intellectual property is the heart of your business.

It is the foundation for the products and services you offer, so it's important to understand how to manage it. Don't let the many myths and misconceptions about IP get in the way of your making sound choices. Whether or not you're aware of it, your business is generating intangible assets which could become the most valuable element you own, as long as you take steps to make sure you do actually own them.

I've built my business from the ground up, and helped many people to do the same, by treating intangibles with respect, and taking advantage of the benefits they offer.

Writing a book inevitably involves a subjective judgment about which topics to include and which to exclude, so it's safe to say that there is a whole lot more to it. I hope reading this book has given you a better understanding of the legal aspects of branding and intangibles, but more than that, I hope it's left you excited about the opportunities that are rapidly emerging for those who have the drive to build a business, and the knowledge they need to protect it.

Appendices

Data Protection Act: privacy policies and your brand

When a site stores personal details there are certain legal regulations that must be complied with – specifically eight principles for the lawful processing of data set out in the Data Protection Act.

Generally, these require that individuals' personal data such as name, phone number or address be used in the way envisaged by these principles.

Individuals have certain rights under the Act, such as the right to ask and see the information a site holds about them – known as subject access requests. The body that presides over the Act and ensures compliance is the Information Commissioner's Office (ICO).

Beyond the Data Protection Act there are a number of other laws which clarify and add to the obligations placed upon businesses when using data.

The Privacy and Electronic Communications Regulations seek to regulate the collection and use of an individual's contact details for marketing purposes. This would cover sending marketing emails to individuals after having obtained their email address in exchange for a newsletter or an eBook.

A key question here is whether the individual has to specifically opt in to receive certain types of communication, or is it sufficient for a business to give them an opportunity to opt out of certain uses it might want to make of their data?

For most forms of marketing, the general principle under the Regulations is that of 'prior consent', namely the individual should ideally give consent to the use of their details envisaged by the business before they can be contacted.

In practice this consent can be sought by providing an 'opt-in' or an 'opt-out' tick box at the point of collection. The difference between the two is that, with an opt-in, the individual gives specific permission, whereas an opt-out means the individual is assumed to give consent unless he or she specifically prohibits marketing emails. Recent EU initiatives on cookies have also been introduced, as briefly mentioned below.

An alternative means of showing consent under the Regulations is through 'soft-opt-ins'. This is where essentially prospective customers or clients provide their details, in order to download an eBook, for instance.

Soft opt-ins have a number of conditions attached, namely: the details should be collected in the context of a sale or negotiation of a sale to the individual; the marketing emails should relate to similar products and services only; the individual must be provided with an opportunity to opt out at the point when the details are collected and every time they receive a marketing email (this can be done by way of an 'unsubscribe' link in the email). For more details on best practice for email marketing see the Direct Marketing Association's guidelines.

For business to business (B2B) marketing emails, however, the above restrictions do not apply.

The opt-in restrictions in article 22 of the Regulations only apply to 'individual subscribers' and not to 'corporate subscribers'.

However, beware of sole traders and partners who are effectively businesses in the guise of individuals. If there are any such individuals in your business database, they need either to be treated separately as individuals, or the whole database needs to provide the opt-out and other facilities required for individuals.

Obviously individuals from companies may, in practice, be providing their personal details, but where, for example, the marketing email is addressed to the company itself and the recipient's email address is non-personal, then no opt-in provisions should be necessary.

That said, every marketing email should always display the identity, contact details of the sender and, if sent by a company, contain the respective details of the organisation such as the company's registration number.

In addition to this, any individual can at any time under the Data Protection Act request an organisation to cease or not to begin direct marketing to them. Once an individual has made such a request, they do not need to wait for the organisation to contact them. The request must be complied with in a reasonable time. Usually it takes time for the opt-out mechanism to be implemented, so it's a good idea for the business to send the individual a brief email saying that the message has been received and will be acceded to, but that it may take a week or so to set this up.

It is good practice for businesses to keep all such requests in a 'stop list', to be run against any future emails before they go out so that, should the organisation acquire that individual's details again at a future date, it does not start sending them further direct marketing material. This particular opt-out is not confined to emails, but may also apply to other types of communication.

Although the legislation sets the threshold of what is acceptable in relation to email marketing, it's important to also make yourself aware of the terms of business of your hosting service (that is, your email service provider) before engaging in direct marketing.

That contract may have even more stringent clauses. For example, some hosting companies may be able to seek damages if your business engages in unsolicited bulk mailing.

In all, best practice for ensuring compliance with legal requirements is by using opt-in based marketing as much as possible, and stating how you will use personal details (for example, by featuring a link to your privacy policy). Ultimately, it depends on the business you are in as to how you comply with the requirements of the legislation.

Businesses must in any event provide individuals with information as to their identity, and the purposes for which the data is sought from the individual and other relevant matter (e.g. if the data is to be passed to a third party), and all this is usually wrapped up in your business's general privacy policy. You can either link your privacy policy to the easy way for individuals to opt out of your emails, or you may put both these requirements (privacy policy and opt-out) in one web page.

If you intend to share data with third parties, or to sell the data, then you need to be careful how you set up your data collection facility, and to ensure that the data stays 'clean' (that is, up to date).

Finally, make sure you have a good system in place for handling complaints about unwanted emails. Failure to comply with data protection regulations could prove embarrassing in certain situations, and could even lead to a criminal conviction.

New regulations in the pipeline

There has been brief mention of the changes to data protection law in 2011 and in May 2012. There are important implications for businesses so more information should be sought from the Information Commissioner's Office at www.ico.gov.uk. This site is worth visiting in order to understand the new law on cookies. Notice that the ICO's site contains a prominent notice just underneath the browser stating: 'The ICO would like to place cookies on your computer to help us make this website better. To find out more about the cookies, see our privacy notice'. Then there is a box that individuals are required to tick if they agree to accept cookies from the site. Otherwise, as is clear from the explanation in the privacy policy on the cookies the site uses, individuals will not be able to view webcasts without having to complete a form each time they want to visit the webcast, and so on.

So your website will need 'terms of use' and a 'privacy policy'. What other changes are we likely to see in future?

Changes to the law on privacy

European legislation designed to increase protection for personal data and harmonise rules across the EU was introduced in 2011, and implemented in 2012.

At the time of writing, anyone who processes personal information in the UK must register with the Data Commissioner and pay a fee. The proposals recommend abolishing this requirement. This will ostensibly reduce the burden on data controllers, but in reality they will be expected to have the registration information to hand, which will bring with it its own costs.

Proposed fines for breaches of the rules are significant, capped at 2% of turnover. For large commercial enterprises the maximum financial penalties for inadequate data protection measures could be staggering. For smaller businesses this is less of an issue.

The proposed reforms require any loss of data to be notified within 24 hours. This requirement has been particularly controversial, as many businesses are ill-equipped to identify and address data losses quickly.

One hot topic is the proposed right to be forgotten, enabling people to require data processors to delete personal information, and also to identify how the information has been shared, if feasible. Increased administration arising from this right, combined with a greater burden to obtain explicit consent, and the training involved, could be very costly for businesses.

The proposals have some way to go before regulations are put in place, and must first be approved by members of the EU and the European Parliament. So, the changes might not be enforceable till at least 2014.

Cloud computing

One further issue to consider in light of the growth of cloud computing, is that personal data must not be sent out of the EU without consent or adequate protection. As cloud solutions often store your company's data in a range of different locations, meeting these obligations can be difficult. This is especially so where you have already collected a large volume of data from people who have not given this specific consent, as you may need to chase each of them for additional permission. However, new solutions are emerging which guarantee that data will not leave the EU, and these are certainly worth investigating if this issue applies to your business.

Glossary

This brief glossary highlights some of the terms used in this book that are commonly confused.

Assignment – A transfer of ownership, e.g. of the copyright or trade mark rights. Under English law, an assignment must generally be confirmed in writing and signed by the person giving up the right.

Community Trade Mark (CTM) – A European trade mark which gives you rights in all 27 EU countries including the UK.

Contract – A legally binding agreement between two or more parties which is in writing, or oral, and the terms of which are implied by law or custom. To breach a contract is to fail to perform the agreement in some way or at all. This might include not finishing a job, not paying in full or on time, supplying goods that were out of line with what was described, and so on.

Cookie – A piece of information stored on your device by a website that is accessible only by that site. However, advertisers can use cookies to track your behaviour if their content appears on pages across the web, giving rise to privacy concerns. European law now requires website owners to obtain the prior consent of a visitor before placing a cookie on their device.

Copyright – If you author an original creative work, copyright gives you the exclusive right to make copies of your work, to distribute it to the public and to exploit it in a variety of other ways. As such it gives the creator control over who benefits from the work financially. The right includes that of being credited for the work, granting permission to make adaptations of it, or to perform the work in public. It applies to any expressible form of an idea or substantive information, and lasts for a certain period of time. Copyright protects many materials, including written, creative or artistic works such as brochures, films, music or paintings, logos, and even computer programs. Some jurisdictions require formalities of registration to establish copyright, but most, including the UK, recognise copyright in any completed work, without formal registration.

Cybersquatting – Cybersquatters buy domain names which include words that someone else has better rights to, for instance because they own the trade mark. If you are a celebrity, a cybersquatter might buy www.YourName.com and offer to sell you the domain at an inflated price, or try to profit by displaying adverts to visitors who expect to find you at that address.

Damages – A claim for financial compensation from a third party whose wrongful conduct, such as breaching their contract with you, has caused you a loss.

Data Protection Act – Broadly speaking, the Act protects the way in which personal information is used, for example by websites that collect email addresses and marketing data. More detail is available in the Appendix.

Derivative works – Adaptations of copyright material, such as a translation or new edition of a book, or a film of a novel, or a performance of a song and so on are derivative works. They attract their own copyright if independent skill and labour are involved in producing them, but the permission of the owner of the original copyright work is necessary, otherwise the derivative work will infringe copyright.

Design registration – If a design is novel and registration is sought in the first year it is possible to protect the visual appearance of products and logos through registration. This gives additional protection over copyright because once registered, it is not necessary to prove copying to establish infringement.

Exclusive licence – An exclusive licence means the exclusive licensee is the only one with rights to exploit the IP within the scope and territory covered by the licence. Not even the owner of the right being licensed may exploit intellectual property that is subject to an exclusive licence. It's therefore important to ensure the licence safeguards the owner's position in the event that the licensee does not live up to expectations.

Fair dealing – This is a defence to copyright infringement in the UK, on the grounds that the use made of a copyright work was for the purposes of private study or research for non-commercial purposes, or that it was for the purpose of criticism, review or news reporting.

Infringement – Infringement of intellectual property occurs when someone encroaches on your exclusive rights under your trade mark, patent, design or copyright.

Intellectual property – Intellectual property refers to a range of rights that the law grants over 'intangible' property, i.e. property that you cannot see, touch or feel. For example, copyright, trade mark, patent, design, trade secrets and other related rights are intellectual property rights that can be owned and transacted just like land.

International trade mark – Trade marks are territorial, so a UK trade mark gives you rights in the UK. While there is no such thing as a global trade mark, there are mechanisms in place under international laws that enable you to register a trade mark internationally, for example by using the Madrid Protocol system to file for trade mark protection in countries that are party to that system.

Joint authorship – This is where more than one person is author of a copyright work. The problem with owning copyright jointly is that, unless you can separate your contribution from that of the other party – for instance if one of you has written two chapters of a book, and the other ten chapters – it would be impossible for either of you to exploit the work without the other's agreement.

Know-how – Knowledge that is gleaned by a business through experience of a particular system or process. Know-how gives you a commercial advantage, e.g. due to your particular approach to manufacturing something, or a finely tuned business process you have developed. Your know-how is a trade secret if it is protected by obligations of confidentiality or restrictions on access to the know-how.

Licence – A licence is the means of granting another party permission to use your copyright or other IP. As owner of the IP in question you have exclusive rights to exploit it, so without transferring ownership you may carve out rights for others to also exploit the IP. For example, you might grant a foreign business a licence to use your technology or brand name in their country.

Madrid Protocol – The Madrid system provides a simple way to register a trade mark in countries which are members of an international system known as the Madrid Protocol. Many countries are party to Madrid. There are several advantages of registering a trade mark through the Madrid system, such as ease of administration, cost savings and flexibility.

Moral rights – Moral rights protect an author's non-economic interests. One of the most important moral rights is the right to be identified as the author of a work. Another is the right not to have a work falsely attributed to an author and to object to derogatory treatment of a work which might prejudice the reputation of an author. In the UK, moral rights, unlike economic rights, cannot be sold, but they may be waived.

Open Source Software (OSS) – Open source software is software for which the source code – something you might equate to a blueprint – is freely available under licence. It's important to understand your rights before using it, as many licences will permit you to modify software only if the resulting product is distributed under the same terms, while others will allow you to make any non-commercial use of the software.

Passing off – The law of passing off protects the goodwill and reputation of a business against unfair exploitation by others. It is a right that protects your business despite the fact that you don't have a registered trade mark. It is necessary to establish that you have rights in the name, or other brand symbols, and that the other party's actions confused (or are likely to confuse) your customers into believing the goods or services were offered by you.

Patent – Only a patent can give you a monopoly over ideas (assuming those ideas take the form of a product or system that is capable of being patented). If you are granted a patent, you can prevent others from working your invention, even if they have developed it independently. To obtain a patent the application must include one or more claims defining the invention, and these must meet the requirements for patentability, such as novelty and non-obviousness. As with trade marks, patents are territorial and protect you in the countries in which you register your right.

Patent pending – A patent pending application is the name you give your patent application in its first 12 months. It is the period of protection you get when you first file a patent application, before you need to take any further steps. Patent applications are confidential during this period, so it can be a useful way to ward off competition without disclosing the details of your application. You can test the waters and abandon your application if during those 12 months you've found it's not commercially worth pursuing.

Privacy Policy – A privacy policy explains how you will respect the privacy of your clients/customers/users. It describes how you will collect, process and share personal information.

Terms of Use – Terms of use govern how visitors can use your website or service. Typically, they will prohibit users uploading offensive or infringing material, using your work without permission, and if appropriate might impose age restrictions.

Trade Mark – A trade mark is a distinctive sign used by an individual or an organisation to indicate that their goods or services originate from them. Trade mark registration gives you exclusive rights to use your sign with the types of goods or services you offer, and is essential to creating and protecting a sustainable brand. Typically, a sign would be a name, word, logo, or strapline, or a combination of these elements.

Trade secret – This is knowledge that you keep secret within your business. Sometimes, keeping an invention secret can be a better option to patenting it as you are still able to exploit its value without incurring the costs of patenting. You could even license use of the invention to others under strict confidentiality obligations. However, if the details of your invention become public the information loses its value, nor do trade secrets stop others from inventing the same process or product independently and patenting it.

Typosquatting – Typosquatting is a type of cybersquatting which relies on registering domain names commonly mistyped by Internet users. For example if your website resides at YourBrand.com, a typosquatter might catch the unwary by registering YourBramd.com.

Uniform Domain-Name Dispute-Resolution Policy (UDRP) – The UDRP applies to top level domain names, and is an administrative scheme to resolve disputes relating to certain domain suffixes. In the UK the system that applies is the Dispute Resolution Service run by Nominet. If a top level domain name you lay claim to is registered by someone who is cybersquatting or typosquatting you may want to try to recover the domains by initiating a UDRP.

United States Patent and Trademark Office (UPSTO) – The agency responsible for the administration of patent and trade mark registration in the United States.

Unjustified threats – If someone else is using your trade mark, design or patent, in an infringing way, in some circumstances you could be deemed to be making unjustified threats by objecting to the infringement, such as if your objection hints at threatened legal action. So, even though you may be the wronged party, by making an unjustified threat (as the law defines the term), you put the other party in a position to be able to sue you for damages.

Further Reading

Abrahams, David. *Brand Risk: Adding Risk Literacy to Brand Management.* (Gower Publishing, 2008).

Brown, Rob. *How to Build Your Reputation: The Secrets of Becoming the Go to Professional in a Crowded Marketplace.* (Ecademy Press, 2007).

Godin, Seth. *Purple Cow: Transform Your Business by Being Remarkable.* (Penguin Books, 2005).

Grant, John, Ashworth, Charlie, and Charmasson, Henri J.A. *Patents, Registered Designs, Trade Marks and Copyright for Dummies.* (John Wiley & Sons, 2008).

Haig, Matt. *Brand Failures: The Truth About the 100 Biggest Branding Mistakes of All Time.* 2nd ed. (Kogan Page, 2011).

Kapferer, J.N. *The New Strategic Brand Management: Advanced Insights and Strategic Thinking.* 5th ed. (Kogan Page, 2012).

Peters, Tom. *The Brand You 50: Reinventing Work.* (Knopf, 1999).

Ries, Al, and Laura. *The 11 Immutable Laws of Internet Branding.* (Harper Collins, 2000).

Ries, Laura. *Visual Hammer.* (Kindle, 2012).

Scott, David Meerman. *The New Rules of Marketing and PR: How to Use Social Media, Online Video, Mobile Applications, Blogs, News Releases, and Viral Marketing to Reach Buyers.* (John Wiley & Sons, 2011).

Sinek, Simon. *Start with Why: How Great Leaders Inspire Everyone To Take Action.* (Penguin, 2011)

Trout, Jack. *Differentiate or Die: Survival in Our Era of Killer Competition.* 2nd ed. (John Wiley & Sons, 2008).

Acknowledgements

I would like to thank the following clients and contacts for discussing their experiences of legal branding with me. The conversations shaped my thoughts and ideas in writing this book: Steve Dawson; Julian Fowler; Will Critchlow; Raja-Saddiq Khan; Madelyn Postman; Nick Sheaff; Julia Foster; Mindy Gibbins-Klein; Aaron West; Emma Mead; Donna Sheehan; Daniel Doulton; Chrissie Lightfoot; Cally Robson; Amro Ghazzawi; Inez and Gus Bodur; and Alastair Moyes.

Many thanks too to Jeremy Phillips, David Abrahams and Michael Harrison for taking the time to review an early draft of the book and give me their valuable feedback. Also to Kathy Gale, who gave me invaluable guidance and referred me to excellent professional editorial support to help me during the writing of the book. Lynda Swindell, Johanna Robinson, Lisa Carden, Jan Bowmer, and Fiona Pike, thank you so much for your guidance and help.

Writing this book has been difficult to fit in around running a busy law firm, and I could not have done it without Stefano Debolini, who provided superb support both in researching aspects of the book, and in reliably assisting in the office day to day.

Last but not least I must thank my husband Paul, who provided solid support throughout the project in a variety of different ways, and my daughters, Chloe and Lilia, whose interest spurred me on to want to complete the writing of this book as a legacy for them.

Index

About the author

Shireen Smith qualified as a solicitor over 25 years ago and in 2005 founded Azrights, a specialist Intellectual Property and Internet law firm dedicated to online brand issues. Shireen's interests are broad and varied, and though her focus lies firmly on IP, Internet, and branding she previously qualified as a journalist at the London College of Printing, has raised two inspirational daughters, and lectured in business law. Having had an international upbringing, Shireen at one time even considered becoming a professional linguist, before deciding on a career as a lawyer.

After graduating in law from East Anglia University Shireen worked both in commerce and industry (at Coopers & Lybrand and Reuters) and in private practice (at Overbury, Steward and Eaton in Norwich, and Eversheds in London), handling commercial subjects like tax, employment law, media and technology law, before focusing on technology contracts and intellectual property during her five years in-house at Reuters. Having developed an interest in the field, Shireen completed a Masters degree in Intellectual Property Law at London University's Queen Mary and Westfield Commercial Law Unit in 1996. Shireen is now a member of, among others, the Society for Computers and Law, the International Division of the Law Society, and the International Trade Mark Association, where she sits on the Internet Committee.

Aside from prolific writing on her various blogs, Shireen's work has been published by the Society for Computers and Law, Caritas, Bloomsbury's *QFinance,* to which she contributed a chapter on cybersquatting, and the recent *Reputation Management: Building and Protecting Your Company's Profile in a Digital World.* Shireen has also chaired and been a regular speaker at conferences held by Central Law Training, part of the Wilmington group of over 16 companies, and a leader in the field of professional education. Separately, Shireen ran workshops at the British Library for two years, helping entrepreneurs to realise their ambitions, and has given a number of talks at the LSE.

Shireen is interested in entrepreneurship, new technology and how the internet and social media are transforming the business landscape. She is part owner of a digital media business with her husband, which focuses on online marketing and social media for professional services businesses.

Lightning Source UK Ltd.
Milton Keynes UK
UKOW03f1302041213

222373UK00014B/506/P